Camino del Sol

A Latina and Latino Literary Series

The Buried Sea

New and Selected Poems

RANE ARROYO

The University of Arizona Press   Tucson

The University of Arizona Press

Library of Congress Cataloging-in-Publication Data
Arroyo, Rane.
    The buried sea : new and selected poems / Rane Arroyo.
       p. cm. — (Camino del sol)
    ISBN 978-0-8165-2716-8 (pbk. : alk. paper)
    I. Title.
PS3551.R722B87   2008
811'.54—dc22   2008032913

Publication of this book is made possible in part by the proceeds of a
permanent endowment created with the assistance of a Challenge Grant
from the National Endowment for the Humanities, a federal agency.
♺
Manufactured in the United States of America on acid-free,
archival-quality paper containing a minimum of 30%
post-consumer waste and processed chlorine free.

13   12   11   10   09   08   6   5   4   3   2   1

To Glenn, always and in all ways, my love

to the brother and sisters Niji, Diva, Anita Josefina, Selena and Little Bee
to Mami, Mike, Marj and familia
to amigos and lovers—living and dead

& San Carlos—someone still loves you

Contents

Ghost Island: New Poems

Poeta Sin Permiso, Poemas Sin Fronteras

On the Work of Rane Arroyo: A Foreword

Luis Alberto Urrea

> *I have waited all my life for permission and learned*
> *there isn't any that matters.*
> —Rane Arroyo

The multi-headed beast known lately as "Latino Literature" has reveled in its outsider status. The very roots of much Puerto Rican, Nuyorican, and Chicano poetry, for example, tap deeply into the marginalized status of the poets and the cultures from which they spring. The amazingly liberating use of code-switching (English-Spanish-Caló-Spanglish) was unmistakably inclusive to those in the outsider club while creating a barrier to those in the dominant culture who could not parse the meaning of such tumbled linguistics. Fire-breathers like Alurista and Piri Thomas set the borders with language: we were outside the mainstream, yes—but the party out here is fantastic.

The mythos of this literature, then, is paradoxical: egalitarian, yet exclusive.

We embrace differences, we champion the underdog, we advocate for witness, social justice and tolerance. We are fighters for justice. We champion inclusion. Well, now that we have Ph.D.s and tenure, that's what we tell ourselves over mojitos at our faculty gatherings.

> *I sing my songs: Gloria, Kyrie, Credo, Santus and*
> *other prayers in my key and I laugh choking with dirt*
> *at the idea that there will be something left of me*
> *to bury later....*

❧

What makes a great poet?

Consider Rane Arroyo. He is the poet with the name that forms a small haiku. Issa might have said of him: *Spring showers/ refresh/ the dry canyon.*

Yes, Rain—a felicitous re-imagining of René. The mystery of great art lies here. Whatever it is, great art is certainly rain falling into a singed and thirsty landscape. To go beyond the mystery of the poet's presence is a reduction. I don't want my poetry without its mystery, and I certainly don't want Rane Arroyo without his. Still, a few words—but not too many....

There is nothing bucolic about Arroyo's ferociously beautiful yet muscular work. The nostalgia that haunted Neruda certainly permeates many of these verses. But Arroyo's eye is modern, and the nostalgia is often slightly regretful because Arroyo is astringently honest. He may be one of the most honest poets working today.

And he stands nearly alone.

There is no exile more pointed than the exile from your own community.

> And it was Puerto Rican drag queens and
> *Black drag queens that started*
>   *the Stonewall riots because Judy dared to die.*
> *The hard part of living alone is*
>   *trying to take pictures of yourself.*
> *Not always in drag. It's always a*
>   *close-up—unless, of course, your arms*
> *grow unusually long....*

The brother just doesn't sound like anybody else in the Latino crowd. In playfulness, in expansive line length, in deftness of tone, in restless attention to shifting thought, these lines remind me more of James Schuyler's urban afternoon light than anything else.

I do not care to make a case for any poet's suffering or struggles. This is beyond the point; besides, if there is any suffering to explore, the poetry should explore it and dissect it. Complaint is not Arroyo's métier: you don't get extra credit in this class for suffering. But we must take into account certain aspects of this literary journey.

If Rane Arroyo does not sound like his peers, can his peers truly hear him?

Are we ready to embrace a strong, gay, male voice? A voice without apologies. A voice that speaks out of turn, with no permission requested and none granted. A voice more heroic than all the blustering clamor around it. Again, I do not seek to define Rane Arroyo, the man; however, his poetry stands honest and revealed. He has never once backed away from this aspect of his identity. (Yes, there are many other aspects—professor, scholar, son, lover, reader, colleague, culture warrior, believer in God, sexual celebrant.)

We might recall how reluctant much of the Chicano/Latino literary community was, at first, to champion John Rechy's brilliant work as their own. Later, much fear of Richard Rodriguez's writing was couched in political terms: he seemed to champion Republican ideas, and the resoundingly Leftist raza were aghast! What, a possibly conservative Latino? This was anathema. Later, when Rodriguez "came out" in his writings, you could hear the clatter of feet heading for the exits. "I am Ariel," he said. "Later, homes!" we said. It took the critic Juan Bruce-Novoa to begin redefining inclusion for us.

How can the marginalized marginalize their own?

> I'm north of my own life,
> on a useless porch in winter,
> a Puerto Rican close to the North Pole.
> I'm Columbus's orphan,
> so often out of place.

Rane Arroyo paid dear personal tolls for standing tall in his own life. It is not my business to discuss these matters—his writing will tell you what he feels you need to know about family and fathers. But it should be stated here that, if the stance of outsider is paradoxically central to Latino literary experience, this marginalized status begins in the home, on the street, in our barrios, on the front porch. Our parents are definitely not Mr. Jones or Mrs. Smith. Our language is not what Lou Dobbs would have us speak. Our accents are not the same as the sound of Main Street. We carry hidden codes within us that don't often translate—brown Madonnas, household saints, ancient songs, odors unsmelled in Cleveland or Kansas City, weird Spanglish conglomerate linguistic markers, tropical memories and histories, humors and lusts and nightmares and sins that are entirely our own.

Arroyo, like me, had another interesting margin, his own small border to cross—he didn't "look like" a Puerto Rican. I didn't "look like" a Mexican, either. Arroyo is not a small, dark, "Latin" looking fellow. Of course, this expectation can be denounced as racist when others do it, but it's a bit of comedy when our own relatives celebrate it.

Add to these factors a heroic struggle with health and illness. You begin to see a formula of sorts, the algebra of a writer's soul. One could fill blackboards with these calculations. All of them anecdotal and simplistic. No formula can truly define a writer of this quality.

But it's a start.

❧

I make the bid here for Rane Arroyo. He is central. He is what we need to strive for in our art. He is not a "Latino" poet. He is a world poet who is Latino.

There, I've said it.

"Island to Island." "The Last Rumba in Toronto." "Dream Starring Andy Garcia." The very introduction to this collection. I could cite 100 poems from this book. They stand among proudly anyone's poems.

Forget everything I've said. You cannot define Rane Arroyo. People have tried to define him forever, and they have gotten it wrong. You can only stand in the storm of this astounding corpus of work and be lit by lightning. Drenched from within.

The work is the thing.

The work is all you need to know about Rane Arroyo.

The work stands outside the center because it is better than the center.

Arroyo is his own genre.

Long may he rain.

Introduction
Some Debts Are Angels

1.

"Selected Poems" is work that makes me feel as if I've constructed cemetery angels to accentuate and bear witness at my virtual gravesite.

2.

Sometimes it feels like a dream that I spent the early part of my life in a Spanish world (long before "Latino" was ever used) within the Chicago of my birth. We stayed in our neighborhood and denied the city; its skyscrapers effectively kept things out and in. We'd drive through "America" behind the sealed windows and the locked doors of the family car. My family and I became translators of culture and language from far away and I became aware of the power of glass. Slowly, I've become shatterproof.

3.

These poems are like icons placed in a personal altar. The sense of the world being larger than my own version(s) of it is evident in the texts I've pulled from the void to be my messengers. Yet, I recall the sources of these poems—the initializing images, the faithful emotions, the lonely languages of the discoverer. Even as an atheist, I recognize the power that is lent to objects by prayers, by touch, by the image finally familiarized.

4.

"Thou—that to human thought art nourishment" sings Percy Bysshe Shelley in "Hymn to Intellectual Beauty." I've learned through homophobic attacks, bruise-less violence in academia, and astonishing men naked in my life that profound beauty is not divorced from the pendulum that we simply call the human heart. It is wiser than we credit it. It spurs the imagination to make sense of what would know us in return. It is not accidental that we call sorrow and joy, when given human form, "the passion play."

5.

I've lied when friends and interviewers have asked me if I have a favorite poem written by someone else. Yes, I do. It is not an epic and yet I know of no other work that magnifies the human mind and soul in such a humble way. It is "Caballos" by Pablo Neruda. He writes:

> *Miré, mire y entonces reviví*
> [I looked, looked and only then revived]

And those ten horses in a Berlin snow of long ago have been made eternal. From a simple moment, Neruda transforms seeing into seeking. Those horses did not need to be witnessed by a poet. It is the poet who has been seeking them all of his life.

6.

Gathering "selected poems" into one book can feel like a botched autopsy. The question is: whose corpse? God's or the poem's? Or just a passing giant's? Mystery thrives with or without approval.

7.

I spent the first days of school not responding to my name. I wasn't Ray, not yet. My favorite name was and is what Abuela called me, Junito. Three vowels, the music of me.

8.

I'm often asked how I describe myself and that answer is easy, even if complicated in praxis: I'm a Puerto Rican, gay, Midwestern, educated, former working class, liberal, atheistic, humanist, American, male, ex-Mormon, ex-Catholic, pseudo-Buddhist, teacher, reader, global, and popular culture-informed poet. These are a few of the adjectives I've come to own and that inform my poems. To my surprise, readers have found me while I breathe.

9.

I think John Ashbery is one of the great comedy writers of our time, one that understands the many ways to feast on darkness. In "The Skaters" he offers this aside:

> None of this makes any difference to professional exiles like me, and
> that includes everyone in this place.
> We go on sipping our coffee, thinking dark or transparent thoughts . . .

The poem continues with this promise, "It all ends in a smile somewhere." I am smiling as I gather my poems—the wonder that it is me doing this, fate's secret darling.

10.

On starting high school, I was placed in the lowest track in English courses. Being one of the few minorities in that suburban school, I was automatically dismissed as an "other," someone of the margins, someone remedial simply by the weight of his name and the burden of his skin and kin color. How fortunate for me. It turned out that my teacher was older, ready to retire and chose to follow her choices of texts instead of the prescribed ones. It was there, in that non-sexy purgatory, that my teacher read Emily Dickinson aloud. I heard and realized that despite my Americanization, I didn't know how to speak English yet.

11.

Over 25 years ago, I sat down at a stripped table in my sexually-charged Chicago and wrote a list of ideas for five books of poems. It was a map, my version of the yellow brick road, news from a secret warfront. By focusing on my Latino world, I found the larger world. It was thirteen ways of looking at a mountain, one that refused to stay still.

12.

Having yet one more near death experience recently, I can confirm that
The Buried Sea has been worth the invisible labor of all these years.
Within these pages are the Reagan 1980s, the start of AIDS, the rise of a
linked Latino identity, the continuing struggle against the tyranny of the
majority—even if committed by members of one's own communities. I do
not want or seek the talent to forget.

13.

I see myself as another laborer, someone who doesn't merely witness
events, but claims them as food for the future. By belonging to no one
group exclusively, I've been fortunately free to experiment, to build upon
tradition and to play the role of that little boy who sees that the emperor
is naked in an ugly way. It is a nakedness profoundly different than being
nude while finding intimacy's pause and feast.

14.

There has been one anonymous review in *Publisher's Weekly* that rings true
to me about my own work: *Arroyo works in a Spanish-language tradition of
larger-than-life autobiographical verse.*

15.

For these "Selected Poems" I had some titles that I tried out first: *Ghost
Island, Dancing at Séances, The Man Who Became A Book, What This
Thunder Brings* (from Madonna's "Rain" song—unembarrassed irony
after irony). Then I had a dream of Hart Crane, that we were looking
at sermonic cornfields. We saw scarecrow silhouettes scattered about a
compass' circle and I said, "They're all dressed as sailors." Hart replied,
"There's a sea buried under us. It will take us with it when it leaves." I woke
up knowing the title of the book—*The Buried Sea.*

16.

The major figure in my dissertation was Carl Sandburg. My initial idea
was to talk about how skyscrapers are ironically patriarchal, that power
becomes evident in the cultural shifts from the lobby to the exclusive
penthouse. I wanted to compare that to the socialism in Vachel Lindsay's
version of heaven and Edgar Lee Masters' democratic cemetery. It was too
large a topic for me and I ended up looking at the emptying of politics
in order for the Chicago Renaissance writers to be canonized. Praise is
expensive and the poet is paid using literature's money that is to be spent
only within its (secret) company town.

17.

How amazed I am to have the calling of poet. No matter what is taken
away or given to me, thought now demands my fidelity. I've stayed inside
comas and, upon my return to this world, read poems for news. Dear
William Carlos Williams knew this. A poem is a living library, a hospitable
planet in black space, a bell waiting to wear the music of motion across
stilled lands. Writers are the carriers of the voices around him or her. We
are writers and readers in dark times when words are correctly understood
as powerful weapons:

> I drop a teapot in my house
>
> and watch it shatter. I'm busy
> packing for the deportation.
>
> These are not days when crimes
> are necessary for judgments.
>
> Green tea seeps into the floor.
> The empty house ennobles echoes
>
> of what will become statistics.
> Looking into my childhood's awe,
>
> I see a stirred niño. For teeth,
> jade. Yet, we've the same words.

18.

Rene Char writes in *The Formal Share* that a "poem is the realization of love—desire that remains desire." I've been naked with lovers and how mysterious they still remain. Once, I was given advice by a famous Latino writer: "Use you in your love poems and remain vague about your inspiration." If I cannot write a love letter to a man, then I cannot write a love letter to the world. And, despite all the opportunities to be bitter, I am dizzy in love with this world.

19.

I declared solemnly that I wanted to be a painter.

"You want to paint houses?" Papi asked. This is not why he worked at the factory so hard to guarantee us a good education and a future "with clean hands."

"No, no, como Picasso," I sputtered.

My parents looked each other and shrugged. Mami spoke first, "Hijo, all those paints and brushes are expensive."

"Besides," added Papi, "paint on the floor might mean that we won't get our deposit back when we move."

The next morning I saw a typewriter in my room! The family could afford paper and ink ribbons. Mami explained several times that the man at the store told her to tell me to make sure to rewind the ribbon, that it was good for several complete spins.

"A lawyer writes," said Papi.

I taught myself how to type and how to compose stories and poems. I had to for I had noticed that after my parents bought me that typewriter, we ate rice and beans for a week—no meat, no flourishes. Suddenly, I understood how poor we really were, and that my entire family had sacrificed so that I could put down in words the daily chaos and its mending. I am still working to pay back the cost of that typewriter; some debts are angels.

20.

I read in tender George Seferis' *A Poet's Journal* this directive: "Among the many ways that there are to study poets, the simplest it seems to me, is the best: to look at what their works show us. And it is not improbable that they show things which we were looking for." Gathering my poems has been a surprisingly difficult endeavor. Who doesn't get in the lifeboat? What is it that I imagine that I've been saying for 25 years? Have I the art to turn my famine years into a generous feast? Who hasn't been loved?

21.

I've never truly been handsome, even in print. Artists around me look like a pedigreed Italian movie's extras in black clothes and expensive pouts. Reader, I predicted and gambled that you would be real, would reel me in from deep space, and would grin at me. When will the world seduce me?

22.

My new work is taking me elsewhere so *The Buried Sea* is a complete pair of parentheses, a full-scale ark with rooms for my many ghosts—welcome Uncle Rachel, Aunt Sylvia, Reinaldo Arenas, Abuela, Papi, Ruben, and the others. Even the living are ghosts—my lover of 25 years, my girls, fellow poets, good citizens, doctors who have pulled me back from the illiterate void. Lorca claims in "The Duende: Theory and Divertissement," that the future contains "Medusa announcing the baptism of all newly created things." Creation and destruction are an old story not yet totally told.

23.

The dead tell the living to live. This simple message has vast political implications. One day, all the sexual communities, and I include heterosexuals too, will leave as a legacy for the next generations these words which will come only after great social change: *You are the heirs of my joys.* Imagine such a world. Isn't this why we need writers—the imagining? I am used to hard work.

24.

Dawn—and I watch my neighbor's above-the-ground pool swirl. It sounds of the Caribbean, the constancy that has escaped my libido and literacy. Who else on this planet—at this very moment—is thinking about how postcolonialism can't shake off its fleas? This blue sky is like a swatch called *Peeled Sea Wave*. I love how another neighbor's small dog leaps in the air to announce it's time to go inside. A birdfeeder spins madly as two lovers share a cigarette. These moments yield to meaning, and yet, the pleasure of seeing also remains and isn't subsumed by summary. It's like the sea. Sometimes I hear it break against my roof. I've heard it call me by my many names, its blue voice uncertain and plain. Sometimes we meet halfway: here on the page.

25.

I've yielded the notion of Eden in favor of imagination's lands and seas. The scars on my body cannot tell of interior scars. Boris Pasternak writes in the poem "The Steppe" (as translated by A.S. Kline) of "journeys into quiet" and discovers a pre-Fall world. For him, the moment is:

> All, drowned in peace, like a parachute,
> like a heaving vision, All.

But he does return to us from that steppe, from that transcendence. How poorer we would be without his songs and tales, the individual moment linked to others to become something larger than the immediate. May my own poems offer something "like a parachute" and that somewhere in the illuminated seascape (or the idea of it), I and Hart Crane and our mermen surface to this world, even if just for a visit.

26.

I do write every day. I do not keep what I write everyday. Rather, it keeps me. Being between two centuries has allowed me to wear masks in the mirror.

27.

I have no talent for nostalgia. That is the secret treasure of El Dorado. No, I prefer the clumsy seductions of the present. Empty pockets and empty hands do not necessarily mean poverty. Imagination has been Homo Sapien's holiest ghost or else Dante and his Virgil would be merely literature. When I was a little brown boy no one suspected that I was making maps out of what I saw, what hurt them.

28.

The most important moment in my life as a poet was when I won the Carl Sandburg Prize in poetry in Chicago, my hometown, on my birthday weekend. It felt as if I was finally welcomed home, the prodigal trickster. It was not I who had changed in order to be read. Or perhaps I had changed as I became more and more myself.

29.

I've always listened to the advice from my older brother, dear James Baldwin: *For this is your home, my friend, do not be driven from it.*

30.

I remember skinnydipping in the Caribbean when I was 21 and how I rose from the black waters to a waiting moon. I pulled it to me, as I've pulled at poems. There have been times when they've pulled me. This then is a book of embraces.

We send the Wave to find the Wave
—Emily Dickinson, #1604

Early Poems

1985–1993

My Tropics

Sleeping naked
in the landlord's
color garden, you lose

the God of the book
opened by winds.
Airwaves offer songs

about crowns and
thorns. The radio
reads your heart aloud.

෨

It's you and me, for
awhile, while Eve is
in the glacial north

dreaming with dinosaurs.
The Caribbean is ours,
coconuts dangling like

hairy suns. Our fall from
grace is a stumble into
each other's blue arms.

1985

Circumstantial Evidence

On Judgment Day,
my mailman will tell
of *Undergear* catalogues

with Cavafy's Mermen
in neon tropical slings
on the ripped covers;

postcards from the dead;
blue gas and other bills;
urgent needs from many

End-of-the-World-not-for-
profit groups; rejections;
and a lack of love letters

1987

Old Checks

Death cab for cutie
—Boy George/Culture Club

Old checks with old addresses
but look, kitty . . . some animal
leaves its tracks on this page

tricked into thinking it is
a field of snow: Let's let it go free!
I'd go out but lately I drink

too much & too often I forget
which country that I'm living
& dying in so why complicate

a taxi driver's life—shall I bribe
Night to stay one more day with us?
Yes, no taxi to the grave yet!

I'll give the moon a blank check!
See how useful a pen is to a poet?
Let's check the vodka—more than

enough. Not like the *old* days
with friends drinking years up
toast after toast—with Mr. "X"

writing his realistic stories
of Napoleon's soldiers storming Russia,
cocks hanging out like dead sheep &

Ms. "Y" trying to sew her legs together
but never turning into a mermaid
like in picture books—& me, as "Z"

the one always joyfully invisible
hurrying home from liquor stores
under the black skies of youth.

1990

Angels Striptease

upon the horizon. Their
silver bodies as brittle

as new tablecloths never used
for guests. Why has

my shadow deserted me?
I walk the wonderful mules

of my thighs around &
around the bedroom.

1990

The Winter Of My Peace

& there is life after sex.
I button my jeans,
pant through the house.

Love turns any bed into
a gondola, any kiss
into a venereal Bop in Venice.

My lover & I go out for dinner
to get away from who we were
under each other just now.

I'm not suspicious that
the waitress or the busboy
works for the tabloids:

Poet claims he's inherited
Shelley's genitals. This city's
snow men want me to melt them.

1990

Juana and Joanna

Juana and Joanna dance in front of strangers'
headlights. Their pimp, who is learning Spanish
at Allegheny Community College,

is without homework tonight. Men seeking men
sit without shirts and nod to songs from new
groups: *The Albino Bats, Deep Sleep, Raw Bed.*

Spring returns to Schenley Park and these two
boys in dresses won't stop dancing because
of their cosmic powers: they are the wind-up

keys to the night, to our planets and stars.
Whether or not there is a god, they blow kisses
to the stars: "Everything deserves our love."

1991

Sex in the 20th Century

Reinaldo Arenas
killed himself in NYC 12/90.
Castro sleeps well.
Loneliness rarely touches anything

beyond itself.
Sure, I've used my open legs
as a forged I.D.
Sambas are just

formal seductions.
Some men are political
with their erections
waiting for us to salute them.

1991–2

The Orange

Amazing, the orange
burns up this gray morning.

So can a man's pierced
ear if something interesting

dangles: Chris has a music
note. It's always the jazz age

during post-puberty. What
doesn't become kindling

when feverish? I peel
the orange, wash my sticky

hands. In the window is
a version of me in the air and

I could be anywhere right
now, anywhere, just for now.

1992–2006

A Chapter from *The Book of Lamentations*

To be drunk with loss,
to dance with death
—Lord Alfred Tennyson, *In Memoriam*

Another man and AIDS. He is dressed
in the look of this world, the burden of

too much Earthly light. He has drowned
in many strange beds, borrowed clouds.

Medicines are itchy cathedrals, crystals of
lies, palaces of pain. Meanwhile on the news:

"We go through 500 boxes of baseballs
during spring training." But spring needs

no training. Hawthorne was wrong looking
for North American ghosts in ruins: look

around us, at the young so unloved while alive.
AIDS is not just a war inside the body or

our deaths end up being our secrets, random
landscapes of ripe corpses, Sodom's ruins.

1993

Rehearsing the Loneliness

Roads burn silver
under headlights—

so he is alive and able to see
tree leafed with lightning!

He arrives to a dark apartment.
Upstairs, the hockey

players are topping
each other (again).

The ceiling is their cradle.
Television whispers of

bodies in a well in Texas,
how a small town soldier

stroked his secret shadows.
Hello moon, he sings, *I'm not*

busy! He pulls silver teeth from
his mouth and plays poker.

1993

Backyard:

Letter To My Dead

I'm easily distracted by
the green peas in their canoes
against the dying light.

Lovers and friends have run naked
through this green, but they've
never once been bitten by

serpents or Guilt, that half-god.
We remember laughing at
our ill-fitting clothes, the ones

put on later, inside blind
cameras. Amigos, winds in
the trees make empty threats.

1993

Litany in Time of Plague

after Thomas Nashe, 1600

A Christ who comes back to the cave to re-
claim his body after three days without
it must understand desire in its
most exterior forms as I do on

Land's End today. I'm drunk with noon light as
I sit at a table without an
umbrella. I brown like a young husband
or one of Dante's sodomites or

perhaps both. A pitcher of strawberry
daiquiris drains inside my darkening
brain and I love the men and women naked
—but for their clothes—passing by. Walt Whitman,

I see you whistling while leaning against
the walls of Seaman Bank. I don't have
the answer why *straights* should read Oscar
Wilde's biography. He did spend most of

his life out of bed. I read in a mag
that Oscar was the first to die of AIDS,
that he caught it from Satan himself who is
now in the rock and roll business of

possessing Elvis impersonators
that rape and kill. We'll have another
pitcher of daiquiris—banana this time.
And there was a time when Eve did reach for

the nearby stars in Adam's hell of a smile.
So does this winking waiter who assures me
that the Adult Punch-and-Judy show tonight
is like "*something censored in* Cabaret"

but I'm thinking about Lazarus. Did
he welcome back the weight of his old limbs?
"*Limbo dancing in the back patio*
during happy hour folks." Why is "*fuck you*"

the worst curse to caress? Christ promises
to come back as a thief but what's left
to steal from me and "*what vain art can reply?*"
A bell rings, a ship's bell, a church bell,

a cash register as I stumble home
after my shadow. He will be my truest
friend in the grave. We must have mercy for
the Lord, mercy for everyone, mercy,

we must have mercy for the Lord, mercy.

1993

from **Columbus's Orphan**

1993

Transparencies

I see / I inhabit a transparency
—Octavio Paz, "Contigo"

Storm clouds and black crows burden
a January sky. A black cat whose paws have
never touched grass is outside with me,
but only on the stoop. No taste of green
for her. A pregnant sparrow perches on
the neighbor's scarecrow. The first bus
falls towards town. One shoulder of a
sleepy mountain's turned away. From me?
A German Shepherd sees me, barks. "Hello,"
and "I don't blame you for Hitler." What ugly
sounds Bluejays make in beautiful
throats. Just yesterday I said, "Isn't it
just fucking charming here? Look, even
a goddamn white church in the wild." I'm
like that: hormones kicked in wearing hiking boots.
Ready for the wild life! What kind of animal
keeps knocking garbage cans over?
Smells of rain make me feel rich, a land-
owner's cologne. How cold my Central
American coffee I didn't help pick or grind. I once
told a lover that Juan Valdez was my father,
that his TV mule was my pet. I seem to
confuse everyone. Many a morning I've stumbled
into underwear thinking, "How did I live through
that dream and where am I and where should I be?"
It's raining. The earth grows invisible.

Caribe Poems

English should be spoken with
a shovel instead of a tongue.
As if digging your own grave
with each phrase: *Hello. Help.*
This is an apple. How much
is a bus transfer home?
The young bleach their black hair
to match their fathers' bones.

෮

My parents are happier
than I am.

They've kissed with
red lips in a blue ocean.

The time of their youths
before swimming to America.

Before my conception
in a suburb of Chicago.

Guests stop by and
music fills the house.

I sit in my room, brooding.

Later, much later,
I come downstairs, and

I'm forced to rumba.

❧

Your eyes were closed, your hands fisted
in case the taxi driver would laugh.
He didn't; he turned on calypso music

until you boarded your plane, first
class ticket back to your lovers.
I rode the taxi around the city until

I couldn't pay and the driver broke me
in bed to break even but I couldn't
lose your kisses or other tastes of you.

❧

Old San Juan

You still wear white
on your houses,
churches and tombs.

You wait for St. John
to open your city gates:
late husband, slow sperm.

Every bar is ready
to become a church, every
whore a dexterous nun.

So what if your prisons
are full of rats, beggars,
pickpockets?

No matter. You're a bride,
beautiful because
you waited so long.

Columbus's Children

I have often stood at the corner of Broadway and Clark—what the poets
of Chicago call "The Crotch of the Midwest"—and I like that because I
have a crotch too—and on that corner I once had a fight with another
Spanish man—tattooed on his knuckles was the word *F A T E*—and I
was dressed in clean clothes—501s and a T-shirt—invisible in a crowd of
so many other people—Americans as I call them—they call me Johnny
because in Chicago that's short for Juan—and I love being lost among
Americans—they smell good—the men smell like sailors working one
of the Kennedys' yachts—sweet as expensive champagne—when out
of the blue a brother bumped into me—and I said excuse you—and he
said that my mother made food that would give nuns gas—and he raised
his fists at me—and I raised mine—and I could just picture both of our
mothers at that exact moment just falling to their knees—suddenly
filled with the need to scrub all the places their children contaminated
with their trembling shadows—and a police car drove by and both of us
stopped fighting and pretended to walk away—then he followed me and
punched me—I said Rico, why are we fighting?—then he punched me
in the mouth because his tongue was his weakest muscle—I saw things
glowing—blue cars stopped before blinking red light—neon slipped off
store windows—the pink lights in the dentist's office across the street
bloomed like electric-roses—and I felt the pain of that very first punch
when I was thirteen-years old—Georgie from across the street—he
was a white boy in a Green Beret suit—his father worshipped John
Wayne—Georgie would spit at me—and one time I realized who had
been smearing mud on our windows—my beautiful mother couldn't see
outside to look at my father's garden—we were trapped in that house—
and there I was thinking about that when Rico hit me again—Rico and
Georgie at the same time—and so I hit them back—and we were dancing
like itchy atoms—my friend I was with yelled hit him back like a Tommy
gun—my friend got scared by my scary face and tried pulling me back—

Rico fell against the garbage cans—I kicked him—my friend kept saying he's a brother—he's a brother—and Rico was bleeding and he backed up—where's your accent—you sound like a citizen—where's your DAMN accent—you talk American—and then he jumped me again—and the Great Ace guard looked down from his window and threw a dime at us—we could hear him laughing—"For the winner and I hope you kill each other!"—how to stop—how to stop—I jumped out of the way— we were sweat dancing—we looked at each other—Rico grabbed his left ankle—acted like he twisted it—Hey he said—you're lucky your mother ate Mexican jumping beans when she was pregnant with you—and then he ran across the street—because the light had turned green and he had spotted a bus coming—I was breathing hard—and Rico turned around— grabbed his crotch with one hand—raised his fist with the other— I grabbed my crotch and raised my fist too—then he jumped into the bus and disappeared—and the fight was over—and my friend put his arm around me—*Ah hijo, hijo*—tears filled my eyes—I hadn't been anyone's son in a long time—not in Chicago, not in Boston, not in New York, not in San Juan, not in Salt Lake City, not in San Diego—and my friend said "Where shall we go Johnny to get coffee—my matador—my Hell's Angel—my cowboy—my cop—my sailor?"—and he went on and on until I laughed—I said I think my adrenaline glands are shot to hell— and I looked at myself in a store window—my eyes were still brown— no one had slipped blue contacts into them—I was still me—I was still one of Columbus's children—Yeah my friend said—Columbus just followed the direction that his crotch pointed him to and look at the woman he woke up with in his bunk—America!—and we walked down the street back to his house—I needed to feel at home somewhere— and the crowd behind us swept our footsteps clean—as if we had never been there at Clark and Broadway—never—never—never—

The Last Rumba in Toronto

Hoarse beggars here demand to be heard.
Then they smell your hands
for the secrets of your pockets.
Who isn't a piggybank?

I'm north of my own life,
on a useless porch in winter,
a Puerto Rican close to the North Pole.
I'm Columbus's orphan,
so often out of place.

My lover and I step out into the street.
He forgets his sunglasses.
We wear our breaths like spent fortunes.

Tonight the Mr. Leather Toronto
will be crowned, king of midnight.
A herd of men in false black skins
hurry into steak houses
hoping to look like what they eat.

I eat my words:
> Seamus Heaney rejected the notion of epiphany in *Station
> Island* because contemporary life has appropriated the
> notion of the pilgrimage into choreographed acts of civil
> wars in Ireland, in Kuwait, in Argentina.

Even as I write this, 60
> Argentinean transvestites are being executed: acts of "moral
> purification."

How much cleaner than the streets of Toronto must the world be?

The American Dollar is 117.8% today.
Soldiers come home,
photogenic heroes.

I had to get away from everything,
nothing in particular.
Just this week,
in Pittsburgh's Cathedral of Learning
a tour guide announced:

"The city has proudly traded in
steel in favor of computer software.
Now our workers have hands as
clean as anyone's in the world."

I'm poor but that's not why my legs are dirty.

Tonight, it's official:
I have my Master's degree.
I'm in Toronto for a view of myself as a Master.
I have to look at myself in a new mirror.

Friend, this is a *celebration*.
Let's go to ChiChi's where
the waitress and five busboys will sing,
>   "*Congratulations*
>   *Congratula*
>   *tions*
>   *Congra*
>   *tulations*
>   *Con*
>   *gratulations*
>   *(Olé!)*

Of course I'm thinking of music.
There are bongos being played on Isabella Street,
there are bongos being asked questions,
there are bongos asking questions,
there are bongos giving out answers to unasked questions.

Our steps drill through the sidewalks.
The beggars look like dying cows.
The streets are full of ghosts in chaps,
in black eyes and disguises of innocence.

Tonight, I will demand
that the front desk
fix the porno channel, because
tonight I'm tired of reading.

I remember a woman
in Chicago who
came up to me
and whispered,

"*Please!*"
On cue
her boyfriend
came up
and put me
on his shoulders.
I became David, Goliath's disco partner.

My head is still spinning.
After a decade begging for this degree,
what am I Master of?
Who is *my* slave and why?

I feel empty-headed and happy.
I've given all I've learned
to the beggars.

Let Mr. Leather Toronto rule his dark kingdom.
Let the bongos bring the sun back from the dead.

I'll survive them all
just as I've survived
the University.

My lover and I are back
in our bedroom.
How real I feel inside
the rumba on the radio,

song spilling through the universe:
all I need to know tonight
is your heartbeat
is my heartbeat
all I need to know tonight

The New Jezebel

She arrived
in your city
from another
country
she's a stranger
and it is so
strange
to Americanize
and change
no furniture
in her flat
—no turn back!—
ah, listen
to her accent
she's not a new girl
by accident

       She's the new Jezebel
       she's learned her lessons well
       the new
       new
       new Jezebel

her neighbors
are so punk
filling up
their lives
with junk
she has licked
the whip
and the microphone
oh God, there is no
place like home
for now she is
dancing in the alleys
and she is
feeling so pretty

The Myth of Puerto Rico

She:
That spent volcano, coral bed of familial cares,
star-burnt island floating in my brain waters,
I'm terrified by it, by its absence being presence,
so that when I think of home, I think of a green hell
smoldering on the other side of a starless horizon,
palm trees being read by winds like bitter books
that should have been burned long ago, but by whom?

He:
It's just a place and it's so very pretty in pamphlets.

She:
I think of my family's bones as needing the rest
of returning, or being returned, in coffins laid like the
eggs of arrogant airplanes, industrial birds whose beaks
part the sky with indifference, as if the Universe
should give way to the business of dinosaur's blood
and body, gasoline, or whatever name you would give
the *energy* required to remain civilized and unaccountable.

He:
It's just a place and it's so very pretty in pamphlets.

She:
We understand our beauty to be the political ache of
achieving poverty, having nothing, even at the end of long
lives, having nothing, not even the sting of rain in our
lungs, or that taste of sea salt on our lips, or a history
separate from the tourists whose monies we burn in our
feverish hands—we fear only certain imposed sobrieties.

He:
It's just a place and it's so very pretty in pamphlets.

Le Mal de Siam

Father Pere Labat in the Caribbean 1697–1705

They're digging my grave, other priests, with shovels
they borrowed from the buck-toothed widow who sees
the Virgin's face crying for help in each pail
of water she draws and so she calls

for hurricanes to wash the Mother off the Earth
... they're digging my grave ... I hear men
groaning under the weight of stones with dirt on
their wrists and hands and necks

from my buzzing bed I stare into black curtains
hung like the bruised eyelids of my guardian
angel in New Europe—Columbus's wet dream
that dried up too soon—as soon as I

was given the death name "Le Mal de Siam"
they began digging my grave, my brothers
of the old Cross, instead of letting me
slowly slip my way out of my skin

to bite my way into the Earth with
my human teeth like one of my slaves
the eleven-year old who swallowed mud
to put out fires in his heart aching

toward his way home but where is my home?
it's not this pot where I empty myself,
more often than I eat or even breathe,
but what is a prophet after all? someone

who knows what someone in one hundred years
is going to feel? I feel seasick being
landlocked . . . I was happy (what a grand
and dangerous word) on the ship here

where I taught sailors to play chess
those 32 pieces poised in a predictable
cosmos . . . here the game is changed
for I know my opponents' sins too well

and these men count on God's great amnesia
to extend to them, unworthy bastards, poor players,
and after one game the doctor said my head had
to be shaved! the volunteers drank and

washed my bald skull in salt water . . .
from the stings I cried aloud which perhaps
I shouldn't have being the holy commissioned
tongue of Jesus in the just recovered world

but I was feverish and yes forgiven
by the men who now dig my dismissible
bed of dust—Brothers! keep digging your way
into the soil where the Son's shine does set

into its Hell . . . and tell me if
a dragon does guard the way against Satan's
name to keep the Earth's lava roses for himself
only? I need some water please and water

for my gravediggers they're naked because
it is hottest today only hotter in the fiery
pool of my brain with its desire for wines
pressed out of the sky . . . what really is

a pulpit's responsibility but a nervous tic
in eternity? ask the Crossed Man I suppose but
always cross yourself first as you look for that
hook in the shark's ancient mouth . . . oh yes

on the ship as we drifted by the Canary Islands
with their devil's dogged 10-foot monsters
in the sea, I knew of course that all knowledge
learned through experience is never forgotten

or digested . . . ask this shark who has
no memory nor repentance for his stomachs' full
of minor pasts: a shoe a man's ring even
the hammer of the lovesick blacksmith

who in his lust for one of his own kind
tried to smash God's skull by throwing his
tool at the moon and ran below deck to watch
me play slow chess as sacrifice quickened

we had to throw our trunks of belongings to
the brilliantly confabulated sea (Jesus walking
on water and demoralizing Neptune) so
we gambled that our old souls were ethereal

light and would not dare God's anger beyond our
comprehension that, like the storm, where were we?
I couldn't help but say goodbye to all I owned:
1 mattress 1 sheet (future burial cloth)

8 pairs of pants 2 habits 6 shirts (to wear into the
New World's old and bitter place) 6 drawers (I picture
God naked in the Garden every seventh day) 12 nightcaps
1 hat (thanks to my slave for hiding it from pirates)

and 3 shoes . . . the Father and the Son did stop
blowing into our sails then I baptized sailors and
passengers with the little wine I had left
and because of my sacrifice everyone else threw

their keys to private liquor cabinets overboard
—save for one man who was mocked in turn by
everyone and how we did toast the wretch
and his wretched love for things of this world—

still my brothers dig! how big are graves?
listening to the scraping songs of shovels, how
painful the sunburns on their sanctified pale bodies
must be? what sins really surprise Heaven?

I sing my songs: *Gloria, Kyrie, Credo, Santus* and
other prayers in my key and I laugh choking with dirt
at the idea that there will be something left of me
to bury later that night it's raining

my grave sits in the mud now I'm half in it living
priests run to me a lightning bolt hits one
of them as I crawl out and cradle him in my black
arms a circle of men are on their knees praying

I paint the cross on his pale forehead with my thin
fingers I give him my messages . . . I let them know
I'm in a new world where they cannot contact me
as the priests begin to carry my winding sheet

in their arms cradling me back to my deathbed
I do not close my eyelids someone else has to do
that as I reach for a dream of this life this
life in the morning . . . I don't know where I am

I am bathed and clothed taken to a funeral yes
my grave is filled with someone else's form
and I live! I meditate on the glory of wealth for
"the poor you will always have among you"

my lungs fill with the smells of rotting fruits
and beached fishes predicting another fat
earthly spring for me and it must come true
and it must not be false as the widow gazes

into her bucket of drawn water to borrow Mary's
mourning expression but all that is seen is
a rusty circle, the only eye remains
the shallow bottom of the silver pail

Voodoo Ballroom

My world is muddy:
dust held together by spit.
Lovers darken on sheets

dried by north winds.
Cigarettes soften landscapes,
mountains of smoke.

I love old photographs
where I look so young.
I must get ready for

the champagne breakfast
paid for by the publisher
of my memoirs, my lies.

People want from me
what I gave away years ago.
I'm their electric matador,

my head a voodoo ballroom.
My days and nights are
as numbered as my ribs.

My Heart

"Do it," yells the man across the street to his motorcycle.
We each meet the day in our own way.
The aquarium with three unspent goldfish buzzes.
Three flies are flying.
Coffee, traceable to dark, wet trees in Central America, cools.
The black cat on my lap hates poetry, even the sound of it being typed.
My skull and the falling stars sing back and forth the songs of magnets
      in heat.
A car with a broken muffler hums along, mumbling answers to questions
      I haven't shaped yet.
What is a life?
Stacks of typing paper wait to be darkened, dented.
On my white wall a photograph of the poet James Galvin
(cut out from the *American Poetry Review*).
Sometimes I want to be:

> 1. an American
> 2. a poet
> 3. reviewed

James looks like a farmboy (Iowa, Iowa, you have more poets than
      scarecrows these fuse-lit days).
How carelessly James sits back on his hips, staring into the camera's eye.
(Imprisoned inside there is the last surviving Cyclops),
and I think of W. C. W.'s lines:

> *the beauty of / terrible faces.*

When my face opens like James's, it is a year later, years later.
Some life is gone.
Only poems remain.
Perhaps a poem that a magazine wanted to publish before it folded
      ("folded," the flight of such a word).

And so the poem is stuck on a roll without a player piano.
Imagination insists on saving its works as a poem, a tattoo, a quilt, an
    essay, or an aside, like this one:

LOVE'S CHILLY NIGHT

an angel's cold hand
irons leaves into
this flat romance

colors distract us
from stems rotting
under our own feet

an angel burdens
our night with
its little laughs

as a derisive white
moon freezes
far from a fire

Even as I type this my coffee is cold; the peasants who picked the beans are
    sleeping; bottles of erasing fluids await their inevitable moments.
I lose this moment.
I'm dancing in the rain with a witch from San Carlos: Botta—is it you?
Her red skirt turns like one solid year of sunsets.
I almost catch her, but I'm back to this moment.
Just in time to send you, my friends, another telegram.
Here, Wordsworth's worthy words.

(I know I will have to bear their cost.)

CLING (STOP) TOGETHER (STOP) IN (STOP)
ONE (STOP) SOCIETY (STOP)
RANE (STOP)

BUT THE WORDS WON'T STOP and what do I owe?

On my desk: a dictionary.
All mine, my mine.

Words like "lacrimator" wait for me,
   lak re mat ar
which means:

> 1. the lake really matters
> 2. the lilac reddens into matters of the air
> 3. the lack of the red mats in the attic

YES!
All of the above and below.

One of the flies has landed on a photograph of me hiding behind
      Japanese fans.
I stare at the fly staring at the me who no longer exists.
I will not exist soon.
I'm here, behind the typewriter.
Men don't split into new personae at the command of flashes.

We can become fleshless though, like the skeletons in Mexican
      cathedrals, guardians of empty confessionals.
In my room, I stare into a smaller box:

> "a brooding young man embraces
> a golden girl whose blue dress
>
> has the words 'forget Xanadu'
> stitched into it while dice without
>
> numbers float in the air suspended
> between a far Heaven and a near Earth

as a black spider crawls toward
the blind moon. A gray feather's

sleep on a blackening hill is
a hint of uncompleted journeys"

My neighbor comes home on his slow, red motorcycle and enters this
      poem again.
The miles hum between his legs.

One of the flies has bitten me.
The black cat darkens all the windows by jumping sill to sill.
The goldfish haven't lost their glitter.
At last, this is my land.
I've learned to speak its language:
America, I give you the power to break my heart.

from **The Singing Shark**

1996

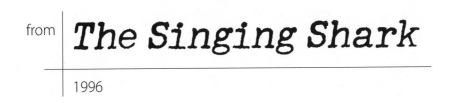

Speedy Gonzalez, Jr.

1.

So what? Who cares that Marilyn Monroe look-alikes o.d.? She was a year of good wine. *Speedy*, a woman once called me. I said, you're not Marilyn. I made her cry. I felt like a rich man, a bastard, Columbus kicking pagan ass.

2.

My mother told me to iron my hair flat like some dumb blond surfer, like a highway in California long after dark. "Imagine, hijo," she said, "you speeding the hell out of yourself."

3.

I'm the best man. I try on a tuxedo, wrong size. I take it off. I'm naked before the groom. I'm his best man but I'm the better man. Speedy, he laughs, don't be afraid. Of what? Why not be afraid? I ache when cartoon animals run and their legs don't carry them away.

Breathing Lessons

Yet another Puerto Rican
Buddhist. He wants to breathe in
peace while keeping his rice-
and-beans cooking skills, his accent,

his blue jeans from the Santana
years, his wine and rum collections
housed inside his head. Today's lesson:
fireflies know they're grasshoppers'

illusory stars. And that
Puerto Rico is only
a comma in Time's poem some
have called the Great Antilles.

The word "greater" is too much ego,
an egg which only revolution
can hatch. Fireflies in San Juan
around El Morro are gardens

with feet and wings. He breathes in. In.
It's the breathing out that is
difficult, for it's a loss. Loss
has, in the past, been his source of

knowledge. If he gives that up, then
loss will no longer be a gain, gains.
Meditation is like a game
of monopoly with his

Latino friends. It always ends
with a coup: the upturned board,
hotels thrown into the air,
useless "get out of jail" cards,

a shower of dollars suddenly
worthless because of the players'
disbeliefs. He feels Puerto Rican
in New York, American

in San Juan, and Catholic
in Buddhist temples. He has blamed
karma for his bad Protestant
lovers. Joy is joy, even if

fleeting, or found when one is
being tortured. Buddha said that.
So did Genet. And Oliver Stone.
So does a fisherman friend who

sleeps with soldiers just to steal their
guns (*In case of an emergency
war*). He isn't the reincarnation
of Che. He must find other
excuses to breathe below his waist.
A teacher warns aloud: *forget yourself,
you are wind*. Is it that easy to let go
of memories, that Spanish entrée?

No more codfish, pork feet, chicken
breast stuffed with chick peas and carrots,
steak with baby onions so it is
Venus wearing a pearl necklace.

He sits and waits not to be waiting.
He sits on toilets, sits on busses,
sits at his desk, sits at lunch
counters, sits in a lobby for

the latest physician who
will comfort him ("No, you're not dead").
He sits in the bathtub filled with tears for
an ancient water god long

evaporated into air.
Baptists once told him to trust that
they would pull him out of the deep
end of the baptismal pool by

his Samson-like pubic hair.
He watches *MTV*'s *The Grind* and
sees men and women reject their
childhood by running away with

their hips. His wet dreams drown him.
He wakes up gasping for air. But
Buddha teaches that most beaches
in Puerto Rico are illusions,

that the naked and the dead are
not obscene but opaque. He longs
for *home*. Longing is thinking so
he takes bigger breaths. In, in, in,

out. He is tired of being
the serpent of the Caribbean
in the tequila bottle. He
is no message floating in

the sea. He has nothing to say. He
is nothing. Nothing hurts his lungs. He
lunges into the Void. But he grows
afraid as he has been so many

countless times when his airplanes
began their descents into San Juan,
urban ghost that embraces
him until he too is breathless.

Imagine The Devil Doing The Tango

His thick tail dragging unharmed
through lava. His raw laughter
and his rude phallus. Joy pours
you a cup of cheer. The feet stop
and the talk turns to Haitian
cemetery architecture. No whispering.
Leaves fly back to trees, tongues
on fire with the light of Eternity.
You screw in a bed that turns
to ash even as you turn under Satan's
widening chest. You climb his
tongue back into your life, your
smoking clothes, your cigarette-veiled
morning. Sunday arrives like a shy
firefly and as sincere about lighting
your way—but where to? You gather coals,
sticks, papers with legal versions
of your names and launch them into
darkness with just one match.
You jump in, bride of light. Unnamed
demons dance on your bones. Your
flesh is real, real enough to lose
in one burst of flames, one grand
blinding wink with your eyelashes on fire.
Just then Lucifer abandons you.
The ballroom shrinks to the size of
a half-note. What exactly is music?

Juan Angel

          Rock & Roll is about work, working at
dreams. Lately I've been trying to visualize
          things. Like attracts like. Like if I
think I might get famous why I'll
          get famous. Juan might become JUAN,
in neon. I'm sure of it. I'm Fame's
          angel. ANGEL. *West Side Story* taught
Puerto Ricans to walk like they're
          suddenly going to explode into . . . a
dance. All Latinos are lovers and
          are required by law to be able to mambo
and samba and tango and salsa
          and do any forbidden dance . . . .
It's as if you have to want to become
          Charo or the Spiderwoman who kisses the
American William Hurt to death. Like . . .
          like they couldn't find one unemployed
Latino actor to take over the role!
          Or were they afraid of giving a Hispanic
the Academy Award? Anyway, it's safe.
          And it was Puerto Rican drag queens and
Black drag queens that started
          the Stonewall riots because Judy dared to die.
The hard part of living alone is
          trying to take pictures of yourself.
Not always in drag. It's always a
          close-up—unless, of course, your arms
grow unusually long. I love
          pictures! I keep trying to choose
the ones that are going to make the
          best album covers. I told you I'm
trying out this visualizing thing.

Like thinking myself into record stores.
Like I can see it already:
          Oasis Records and a fan looks up, spots
me. Screams. Fans start chasing
          me. ME! Like what happened to the
Beatles in *A Hard Day's Night*. I'm
          running and running so my fans don't
catch up or lose me either. It's
          a delicate balance. I mean—look at
Elvis's ghost. It can't haunt
          Graceland in privacy. God gave me my
privates for a reason. I've been
          practicing! For the video shows. I
not only know how to lip sync,
          I hip sync! I'm good in my empty bed:

                              Hello I'm blonde
                              Goodbye I'm brunette
                              After two vodkas
                              You're easy to forget
                              Hey you I'm easy
                              But man you're sleazy
                              Sure I want everything
                                  Everything
                              That has a sting
                              I have to feel it
                              To make it real
                              I have to feel it
                              I have to feel it

Oh, once I started a band but
          all of us wanted to be the star power.
When the neighbors called the cops
          we told them we were on *Star Search*.
Fame! I'm going to live forever.
          I'm Juan Angel. I'm keeping my name.

I mean people know Gloria Estefan.

Trini Lopez. Rita Moreno. Julio Iglesias
showed up once on the *Golden Girls*.

My mother was born in the same village
in Puerto Rico as José Feliciano.

A sign! That I'm Juan in a million.
Juan-derful. Juan is the one. Juan toss
of the dice. Juan chance of a lifetime.
Juan-na dance! Gotta dance!

I'm the Juan and only Johnny Angel.
Oh, Johnny, boy, man, Johnny-come-lately.

Out of my way Madonna. I mean, why did
she get the #1 hit, *La Isla Bonita*?

Barry Manilow and that *Copa Cabana*.
Father used to sing me to sleep with
La Bamba. Why didn't I record it first?
I dream big, but no matter how big I
dream I'm smaller than life, smaller.
I'm tired of waiting for the big break,
the big man, the big boys, the big game.
I'm tired of waiting. Reminds me of
that old Spanish joke about us that
while waiting for a new life in
America we're waiting on tables.
I want to be in America. *Born in
the USA*. See you on an album cover
near you. I'm Juan Angel. Hola, hello?

My First Novel

The poet understands that behind the logical antinomy
the heart has taken sides
—Antonio Machado

There is the sea

a priest steps out of the water as a shark snaps at his shadow

there is the sea
and the burning moon

a drag queen extinguishes the sky with glasses of ice and blue gin

there is the sea
and a gossiping moon
eying white gravestones

a reporter warns an addict that someone will escape through his asshole

there is the sea
and a sailor who is without
cigarettes in a cemetery
overgrown with moonlight

a poet stands naked in his green garden grateful to be growing blind

there is the sea
left to the moon's abuse
while the sailor sleeps

a thief in prison sleeps so much in the sun that he shits gold coins

there is the sea
and a drowning moon

a student sobs that in the movies the wind can freely enter any town it wants

there is the sea

a sailor returns to the mermaid who has promised to eat his heart

there is the sea

there is the sea

there is

here is

here

he

Existentialist With Conga Drum

I love Desi.
In America, north
of the equator,
his name is Ricky.

Ricky marries a redhead
on black and white TV.
When his son is born
he is in voodoo face.

In the father's
waiting room he is
grabbed by the police
for scaring nurses

with his painted
cannibal teeth.
Little Ricky comes out
of the camera's womb.

❧

The sky falls into
my crib and my skin
isn't as blue as my mouth.
I taste air,
swallow it, float on my
screams toward tomorrow.
Eternity can't crush me.
It's jealous I have form.
I shake my rattle,
God's bones.

Desi hits the drum.
Or is it Ricky?

Hollywood is hungry
for his Cuban bones.

It's not magic he needs.
What he needs isn't business.

Lucy is American
except for her
choice of lovers.
How brave this Mother
of Multiculturalism.
Ricky and Lucy don't think
of their bodies as islands,
but that's what they are
in Hollywood swimming pools.

Lucy refuses to be
the Mother of Heaven.

Ricky weeps until there are
enough pearls for tourists' necks.

Cubans chew sugar cane
on the road after revolution.

Lucy likes to anger Ricky
so he spews Spanish like a volcano.

Time is a terrorist who casually
straps bombs to his testicles.

Before life on Earth, there was death.
Death had nothing at which to laugh.

❧

Lucy is in disguise.
Her breasts hide among plums.
She joins *turistas* with cameras.
Tranquility is lost,
like the waters in the moon's
Sea of Tranquility.
Ooops, wrong sitcom.
Havana glows in the dark
of 1950's United States.

❧

Ricky is an orchestra leader.
Between the legs of his band
are instruments to tame
the beasts of Capitalism.
The white patrons dance in white
tuxedos surrounded by white orchids.
Ricky can't lose his accent, or
Havana will wilt in his mouth.
He is a crooner, moon-scarred lover.
This Castro-fleeing cocksman,
defrocked jock, is forced
to take up sing-song in Miami.
He marries Technicolor Tess
of the d'Urbervilles
a.k.a. Miss Liberty.

They become lovers, naked
in the minds of suburbs,
trailer parks, and gossip columns.
He has the goods: Desi
desires a destiny
and he is damned with one.
He can't keep his pants on,
swimming in beds, trying
to escape shark after shark.
He has never left Cuba.
The FBI wants him to kill Castro.
Cuba's Casanova hasn't diddled
Hoover, who is enraged that Castro
stares up America's loincloth.

❧

Lucy hums "Happy Birthday"
to herself hoping
to break strangers'
hearts and piggybanks.

❧

No Latinos play Little Ricky.
He takes after Lucy.

She is white and red,
like a cool drink in any Hilton.

The son of the television gods
is attractive, the way

a wreck attracts strangers
and the strange media.

Maybe I'm not Little Ricky.
Maybe Reinaldo Arenas was.

He was just like Big Ricky:
fucking, fucking, fucking.

Pleasure is a strange god.
It rejects familiarity.

Ricky with Reinaldo as a son
could have turned constellations

into strip shows, something
for every sex and species.

The ache to love too often proves
to be just an ache, an acre of air.

Reinaldo, return to your novels
and to your rat poison suicide.

I wept upon hearing of it, that
you left me as heir to Nothing.

Cuba, don't stop being real:
But then Art makes as many promises as it has holes . . . .

❧

Lucy goes to her first
Catholic Church.
She picks up a saint's bone
and pretends she is

the baton queen of New York.
She puts the bone
against her nose.
Now she's a cannibal!

How cute! She is a physical
actress! No confessions for her!
Scriptwriters follow her
to the end of the 20th century.

An *I Love Lucy* TV marathon.
This life's karma tires me out
but it's Valentine's Day morning.
The cat pisses in her private boxed beach.
God, send me a blue jay, or UFO.
Or any sign, signal, signed studio photo.
I'm tired of painting myself nude,
as if my nudity is the mystery.

This room is bone white,
foam white, Ricky-Ricardo-teeth-white,
Moby-Dick-the-sperm-whale white,
Claude-Van-Damme's stomach white.
H's sexy, in a neo-colonial butch way.
This is a new world of snow, peopled
by snowmen who can't salsa:
"I refuse to limbo under zero degree's line."
Queer to quote myself. Charles Henri Ford
did the same thing during my visit to his
dark Dakota apartment. Indra served us tea
before taking our pictures, turning us
into statues without a garden.
Like Ricky, we live in constant exile.
A republican tells me that there is nothing
romantic about Cuba so long as Castro
blows Gabriel's horn out of his asshole.
He imagines southern Florida as a nest of
killer bees, blue with the hunger for home.
Anne 2 reads Foucault ("Not for fun.").

On the TV, Desi and Lucy pretend to be
Ricky and Lucy. He covers his ears
so he doesn't hear his wife mother him.
The laugh track can't be translated.
It's white noise, only darker.

～

I'm an existentialist with conga drum
tom-tum tom-tum tom-tum
tom-tum tom-tum tom-tum

I love Lucy now isn't that fun?
tom-tum tom-tum tom-tum
tom-tum tom-tum tom-tum

The earth is old but I am young
tom-tum tom-tum tom-tum
tom-tum tom-tum tom-tum

Revolution doesn't need gum
tom-tum tom-tum tom-tum
tom-tum tom-tum tom-tum

The hanged man dances like he's hung
tom-tum tom-tum tom-tum
tom-tum tom-tum tom-tum

Lovers, conga before you're undone
tom-tum tom-tum tom-tum
tom-tum tom-tum tom-tum
tom-tum tom-tum tom
tom-tum tom-tum
tom-tum
tum
tu
t

My Transvestite Uncle is Missing

Questions
I remember you so Elvis Presley-thin
and ever about to join the army (*now I know
the whys of that*), and I remember remembering you:
before breasts, before European wigs, when
the etc. of your sexuality was a secret,
and you babysat me, and we danced to Aretha,
and you taught me to scream for the joy of
a song on the radio ("Romeo requests this from
his grave!"), and I can't call you, what's
your new legal name? Is it in the phone book?
Are you that official? I've heard you're
dead, call me collect please, I'm on my own,
and Uncle Rachel if you were here tonight I'd . . .
I'd sing to you: "pretty woman walking down
the street of dreams," and you could tell me
that story again where gold is spun out of straw

Answers
News of your old death, first I danced in the shower with clothes on,
cracked my green head against a corner, gave you a bloody birth in my
mind, gave myself a satisfying scar, watched an Annie Lennox video where
she has a red towel on her head, I mirrored her, white towel to stop the
bleeding inside my own nest of a skull, then I screamed and screamed, but
the police never came, snow fell from the constellations, everything was
on fire, fast forward, tumbling and I stupidly read the *Song of Solomon* for
comfort, my eye filled up with blood, I strapped a big bandage around my
head, I'm a poor man's Wilfred Owen, I'm my own damnation, you're dead,
I won't sing at the funeral that took place without me, the sun will hear my
confessions, my naked body on a rooftop, cruel cock crowing as if another
ordinary morning, and it is, I did survive, I, someone shows up to make
sure I'm not in a coma, I'm not, not with all these memories, I touch myself
as if I'm still loved, Uncle Rachel, does Death look sexy without a fig leaf?

The Singing Shark Dream, or Toto, I Don't Think We're in Tegucigalpa Anymore

I'm a shark
        no, not a metaphor
                no, not an allegory
I'm a shark
Doubt it?
Put your hand near my mouth and gain
        a belief the hard way
I'm Maria's &
    Tony's son, born after *West Side Story*
                became another Hollywood story
my father was once a Shark lover
a gang member
—his, a theatrical choice
                        y Mami?
she was a Puertorriqueña
famous for
        wearing a white dress to a dance
                oh, spotlight of purity to
                        the itchy stomping white boys
well, one, Papi,
        if he and Mami had finished
                high school before it finished them
                        before reading *Romeo & Juliet*
                        before living & dying it
why they'd get the hell out of heavenly Nueva York
go through the Lincoln Tunnel
        (the United States's asshole:
                "everything and everyone passes through it")

We, the other sharks, the sons and
daughters of other tragedies—what
you think? I'm all alone? There are
lots of other half-humans and half-
sharks—we don't like poetry but
root for Mami and Papi every time I
tell their story, a three-hour dance, a
three-hour dance. . . .

Mami never told her Tony
she got pregnant and it was too late
        to do that because Papi was one
            beached, stinking Shark-loving Jet on
               that infamous basketball court
Mami went mad
            Manhattan turned into Puerto Rico
her rich port of suddenly
          unimportant poverty
how Mami María grieved
        for her dead
shark hungry lover and so I
          slowly took the shape of
her memories in her womb
         and when the doctors
pulled me out of Mami's
         body they first saw
my back fins and dropped me
        into a water cooler
so I thought Earth was
        bluer than it was on the outside
I was smuggled out of
        the hospital and hidden in
the Central Park Zoo
        how clever to hide someone like me
among sharks among my kind

but they THEY tHeY ThEy TheY they forgot
I'm human, that I can remember some
of what is memorable
so Papi is a dead jet
crashed airplane
hijacked hard-on
and Mami is redecorating her breakdown
I send her a message:
a big aquarium for me, please
So I watched white children
in children carriages
being children
to their parents
and they learned to walk
and I learned to walk
in my mind at first
stumble after st-
umble
I did walk after closing time at the zoo:
María's and Tony's freak son on two fins
not so strange
since humans
did swim out
of the sea
and learned
how to stop
gasping
beyond foam,
beyond waves,
beyond the wetness
of the pleasure
of being

so Mami was my cosmic shortcut in evolution:
hey, I'm with the band

I'm a shark
with a man's mind ever so hungry, ever with
an ancient eye fixed
on God and Satan,
skinny snacks, my motto is
have teeth, will travel

Oh
yeah
I
can
sing
1. *La*: a note that follows *So*, or *La*: def. art. fe. sing. the.
2. *La*: obj. pron. her; it; you. 3. *La*: m. MUS. la, A.
Think of my parents
where I come from
Think the rhythm of water
against my brain at birth
and since
while learning to walk I listened to sounds around me, guarding against
night guards, I heard car radios, televisions, jukeboxes with bars, drunks
whistling, televisions, walkmen, walkwomen, commercials in the air,
surfers rehearsing commercial cues, Zorro vs. the Energizer bunny, shoe
songs, slow heartbeats

I can sing
I can dance
I can be funded:

Anger
just leave it on the hanger
no, I'm not angry anymore
danger
don't pick up the stranger
Baby let's f__k

then let's rock
to sleep
I'm the dream that you can keep
I'll rock you to sleep
all night long
this is our song
Baby let's f__k
then let's rock
rock
rock to sleep
You're the dream I can keep

Does the N.E.A. know its ABCs yet?
F is forest
U is utility
C is for clock
K is comely comic
U is for unity

Hello *MTV* this is your singing shark
                              son of Tony and María
you know other sons and daughters who sing their way into identity
I like what Tina Turner says about the movie based on her life:
                    I lived it so why see it again?
That's how I feel
about *Jaws*
West Side Story is a video of my parents'
honeymoon
or lack of one
I'm always aware of *absence*
—isn't that a way to define hunger?
I'm not human
I'm not shark
I'm not a moral lesson

                although maybe there is a poem
                        waiting for you with your name
                                inside my ancient mouth but beware
snap snap says the Mambo Mouth and RuPaul
and Mami snapped
                        and jumped off
                        Hart Crane's Brooklyn
                        Bridge so she could
                        remember what she had
                        forgotten and I lead
                        a fish guard all the way
                        until she sank at the
                        bottom of the Earth
                        and her hair waved in
                        the water like a mirage
                        but it was her as I should
                        know having come from
                        inside her and so Tony
                        and María are happy without me
                        again and I swim away because
                        what else is a shark-boy born to do?
Eve
        was
                buried
                in
                        the
                                Red
                                        Sea
                                                and
                                                        her
                                                blood
                                        makes
                                it
                        red
        —great wave!

78

I'll be on tomorrow's *Oprah* or *Telemundo*, I can only write an
autobiography on water or on gin, no, I don't expect a musical based on
my life, I'm a Puertorriqueño without perspective, I'm no *Grease II*, so
what is life and death about as a shark, not so different from your life and
death, food and sex, sex and food, needs, interview me and I will just
say: *yo tengo una tía que toca la guitarra*, although I have no aunt and no
guitar, I'm blowing you off without tasting you, swim away from me boys
and girls, I'll be a television series soon enough, *seaQuest*. I'm one of the
unloved, made during lovemaking, but some bodies have dark waters
in them so I'm a singing shark without confidence that my future killers
will follow the musical's etiquette: sing before killing, I expect my freak
birth to lead to my freak death, humans love the parenthesis and doors
and illicit affairs, *en voz alta*, I'm on low cruise speed, but what if I'm not,
what if I'm what you waited for,
la voz del mar nunca se pone vieja,
                              or old sea, new waves
Oh Mami and Papi,
I'm a musical without a hit song:
you, and you, and me (No *Tea For Two* is it?)
                    but you're not here
                              but you almost are
            you have salty margaritas because you can't sink
I drink Bloody Marys because I can't pray
                how lovely to be stupidly drunk and mean what
you say: my heart is a piñata,
                    I'm a shark,
                              both things are true,
I'm thirsty for simplicity:
                    Life, you sing to me!

from  **Pale Ramón**

1998

Homesick for America

Tonight, I'm your sailor, Chicago,
a sea-orphaned one who will drown

you in my saltern legs. I feel old in
New Town, new in Old Town, down in Uptown,

an imperialist in New Chinatown,
poor on the Gold Coast, a giant in

Little Italy. I run into Charlie
and his dog *99* who are late for

the New World James Joyce Symposium
on "*The Dubliners* and Place"; bow wow

to you too and bring me home a buzz
bomb souvenir of soluble ideas.

Chicago, let's spend my shore leave
(*what shore am I leaving?*) in

a skyscraper bed with an unlocked view
which Columbus never saw from his

lonely masts. Make me close my eyes;
perhaps I'll tell of the architecture of my

bluing body with yours: *home?* Sí, see, sea.
Lakeshore Drive, I too have stories.

Caribbean Braille

My blind father doesn't
want a volunteer
reader to describe
someone else's depluming.
He'd rather spend his rosary
time remembering, but
what does he long for in his
short attention span?
He has been reflecting
upon the color *wine-red*,
the idea of it in the world,
wine-red as wine and red.
The last thing Father saw
before his eyes burned into
industrial nothingness
was a nova in the shape
of a rose with hot thorns:
my eyes burst into flames
without warning. In his
youth's Old San Juan,
the norteamericano hotels
had roses and wine on tables
which he'd spy on from
cobblestone streets. *Who needs*
fiction? he asks, sure that
I have no answer, but
the son reads his father
to sleep. We wake up in
the morning, compare
mosquito bites. We laugh:

how silly to think someone
might send us love letters via
Caribbean mosquitoes. We
read this Braille by rubbing
our hands over and over
the bright bites. Our bodies are
the books we cannot read.

The Inlanders

For us without a convenient sea,
we have faces instead of boulders
against which the sea breaks, faces that
bear the news of *blue*. Step into any

bar on Halsted Street and the jukebox
offers any stranger: an alphabet
of sound, a language of light,
sentences of foam and current currents.

Enough drinks and you will be thrown against
an invisible shore, will drown in a womb
older than your mother's. You will wake up
with your head as a newborn island.

The Exile

This night train bears the burden of human
imagination, this train of sound, this train of
the song of cold miles. It is your sea, Neruda,
returned on wheels. Black hills in the midnight
are the geography of loss easily crossed and
re-crossed by this business of engines. Cargo
of sand, stars, seas and secret tides pass by us
without directly touching us. Our home of
human bones is crowded with the breaths
of new moments. The heart rattles as trains blur
past; the past keeps unfolding as if the present.
This train is merely a flung seashell with old
laughter in it, when the sea was eternal and ours,
when it was peopled by mermaids and their leviathan
lovers. The train is going and I'm running behind it
while carrying the heavy luggage of breath.

World Citizen

Charon doesn't know a Cuban
from a Puerto Rican.
They are all firewood to deliver.

They're as dead as everyone else.
Charon throws passports and visas
into the bloodied river.

He strips everyone upon landing;
then they truly disappear into
God's dark imagination.

Charon rows back to us who,
while waiting for him on shore,
argue as if countries exist.

We're naked without our flags.

For Selena

In the song book of the dead,
you're the chorus girl who
never gets her Broadway break,
the understudy whose
understudy becomes the star.

That's not you on the T-shirts,
mugs, videos, anti-gun
posters, number 18 of
the year in the childish adult
contemporary music chart.

Tex-Mex angel, your fame is
about your motel-gunned corpse.
For now you're safe to be sponsored
by soft-skulled corporations.
The Mexican Madonna sings

María to sleep while we stay awake.
The prayers of the poor are your
lyrics, Selena, the serene.
We are still without advocates
on Earth or most of Heaven.

Pray for us, hermana, who
must use clock radios to go
to jobs that assassinate us
so slowly that no one believes
our ancient cries for help.

In Amherst

Why is a brown man like me interested in Emily Dickinson, that white woman in a white dress in a white house in a white town?

La loca at this side of Tornado Alley, nun with 50/50 vision.

Sister to Pegasus, she is the quietest breather in any anthology.

Daughter of a Political Demon who wanted to tattoo the eyelids of his son, grandsons, the very-great-grandsons with the word 'Mine'.

She's a bad *Victoria's Secret* poster child.

She's Marla Maples but with preferences for pens and pencils over billionaires who know penicillin by pet names.

She's a pre-MTV icon, secret gypsy, Higginsworth's personal cracked Easter egg.

She's Lavinia's best friend if only through the fever and web of blood ties.

She—whose poems are "The Yellow Rose of Texas" if sung aloud, those postmodern hymns—barely travels beyond her moonlight of clothes, private mind mountains in the neighborhood's void.

Her bed maps of *nada* are detailed, but merely phantom lace turned into maps or cold semen, the imaginary as real and vice versa.

Emily, I'm not a notch in your virgin bed; you can't make me pure for I'm the brown boy in leather in hushed Amherst (*name of a new cartoon series?*).

I grew up with bullets for birds.

You have no Master?

Count yourself lucky. I read your book to find at least one letter addressed to me.

I'm the next rocking robin out of here, back to my rouged streets filled with singing cars, dancing gangs, poetry that should get written down, as yours was.

Attempt at Optimism

Only one person in Youngstown looks happy—
a Mexican girl running ahead of her parents,

feeding her shoes to the gutter, laughing
at the silly engineering job of her hands.

The rest of us are hungover, tired of movies
where ex-lovers show up in trailers for pornos

shot in trailers. Let's follow this young girl to
the 21st century. Too late! She's turned the corner!

The Youngstown Poems

1. Among the Abandoned Whites of the Rust Belt

I love that Jesus was a carpenter
although jazzy scholars now suggest

he was a joyful bricklayer.
I was one once in Mormon Utah

but that winter was so cold that my
celestial toes swelled into twisted claws;

isn't labor holy? The times when I
don't know how to fix something in my home,

I wish I went to miracle school;
water-into-wine is indeed a skill.

It rained just yesterday and my gutters
leaked like fast light through a floating island's

rooted rain forest. A diamond priest
who is my drinking buddy in this

beers-and-shots Babylon asks me
to think about Christ's hands being as

calloused as any communist organizer's in
the American 1930s, but like Paul

Simon sings: *Why am I soft in the middle
now?* The middle-class has always dreamt of

soft beds, soft lighting, software by which
to both forget and to remember their

IOUs, ah, their roots. But we are not plants,
plants are where people work. At least one god's

son understands labor, unlike Buddha
who was rich and so had the mistaken

idea that sacrifice, self-denial and
self-destruction was the same as work

without end, or bills without end. Jesus
had to work hard for his vacation

in paradise. The daily unfortunately
is the eternal. And the nightly also.

How often Andrew Carnegie
is a vampire who visits me without

an invitation. *Goddamn you*, I cry out,
I pay my own rent! Get the hell out!

2. On Seamus Heaney Receiving the Nobel Prize in Literature

I dropped the dish I was swishing in
the metal-rich tap water of this dead
steeltown. What can break in a broken

galaxy? The radio gowned your
verse in imperial lace.
I recalled your face in Pittsburgh,

that suburb of Hell where
every day everyone worked at
salvation even while knowing

there wasn't any left. Your face told
of other readings, seedings that
mostly untook. Booked up as an

Irishman, you read in a sobering
voice that disappointed the dead
drunk. Now, aging in Youngstown,

where my students call poetry prose
because plot is what they know best in
their have-not lives, I'm my own Station

Island. Ghosts weigh my head to see if
I'm a good host. The Christ of Food Stamps
and Malt Beer is damn dry stuff in these

thirsty times. We cannot afford
to bring you here, not even before
yesterday, before the puffed prize.

You belong to the world of clean hands.
Beware what happened to James Baldwin:
lawyers sent his books as gifts to

idiot clients. I sit down in my
post-industrial Victorian home and reread
'Digging.' It's obvious, in terms of plot;

it's the language that has got you that
leeches a silence in me. In these
days of poets, it's your poems I praise.

3. *Betrayals of the Dead by the Living*

I mop the house with the moon's wig. But if
X were visiting, I'd stack my bills due, comb
the chairs, cook something that I'd serve Marx

or Freud or Kahlo. X equals nothing,
now. Cats follow me to the attic. More
paintings, some whose titles are wrong.

It's Muhammad (Ali's) birthday and
James Earl Jones', black voice of black space.
Buttermilk Ranch dressing is no longer ranched.

My true friends will be born after I'm worm
tacos. My new astronaut haircut is just too frank.
Cream suppositories are on sale, and

why not grow old? Motown séance, not my
choice: "Baby love / my baby love." An imprisoned
Shakir wants mushrooms and onions on his pizza.

Hot child in the city in which Billie breast
feeds the masses; that's how it is. Sponsors
seek coffeehouses they can regulate

into missionary positions that
bore them. Too much *Eugene Onegin*?
I now bring books to funerals. Sean is

a dead student, shot in a park; tears are falling
in this poem, but who will believe me?
Oh, Sun, it's you. Students shouldn't die before

their teachers do. You shrug, sell me new days.
I'm tired of the joke: are you growing old in
Youngstown? This is a city of sirens: police,

ambulance, firetruck. Not one is a sea siren.
My X is a dream without a soundtrack, lyrics.
Even now, I can't name you. When I join you

in death will Nothingness still be our chaperone?
You were my best friend in bed; I've diaries
to prove that. What better read in a snowstorm?

4. A Personal Apocalypse

Roofers hammer constellations
into the ceiling. Where is the cat
hiding from this hammer storm? No,
Diva is dead. These then must be
angels clawing through the roof.

~

Found Poem
I reject goldenboy Keats' negative
capability: nothing is nothing.
My cat is in the world, of it.

~

A diva on the radio
and Diva is only
45 minutes away if
I'd drive 68 mph.

Nostalgia is my
sworn enemy but
how Diva would sleep
in the zero of my lap.

5. *Children of Steelworkers*

They cannot stop from writing of Paris in these steeltown coffeehouses.

They quote Sartre, Proust, Genet even as local unions
strike for health care.

These young writers' Christs are not hoddies, tool carriers, shit house
      scrubbers up and down the Ohio turnpike.

No, they possess the French new wave film gift of photogenic sadness.

In the name of messiahs with accents, these poets eat garlic bread sticks
      and swallow wine-on-tap at the *Inner Circle*.

France can only teach you how to turn ruins into tourists spots.

Island to Island

1.

If I sleepwalk in Reykjavik, will I
           wake up on an ice floe that melts from my fever
for travel? I try to sleep in a city
           so close to the North Pole. Airplane vodka
is just a road show. Better to shower
           and take an unshaven look at streets from
my mini-bar in Hotel Holt. After
           Auden, Iceland hasn't often appeared in
our letters. I'm hungry for music, for
           nights when I'd put on my Tom Cruise codpiece
and rock & roll in my Keatsian anguish
           on dance floors that have mapped my desires.
Arriving at noon is odd: not a time for
           sleeping or waking. We go for cream of
white-fish-demon-from-the-depths-of-the-sea
           soup at a Nordic café which turns out to
have an attic that on weekends is a Gay
           bar. No Bjork, just American Blues.
It turns out modern Vikings are mad for jazz,
           the darker side of America
that has always been mine. "I'm tripping,"
           I write Ms. Diane Williams on a postcard
(Sister-black-jet-settee-sitting-beauty),
           "Twin beds in Europe are for 3/4 of
a person." Even the mannequins here
           are Hitler Youth wannabes. Despite their
best black wigs, Icelanders are still blond.
           Back to the room, back to the business of
dreaming about reality (Plato,

I don't need your advice, gracias): *The streets*
of Old San Juan are narrow, dark, scarred by
　　　　　the passing of empires. It's your eyes,
Glenn, that I follow to our century.
　　　　　I sit on the porch and stare at a city often
just imaginary to me. You unpack
　　　　　a novel about vampires in heat.
San Juan throbs like a needle tattooing
　　　　　a scared young runaway. What is his choice
of designs? Why this one? To be worn
　　　　　forever? Then I wake up on the wrong
island. It's dark on the still-green Iceland.
　　　　　Blue winds head toward Greenland's ass, weather
report for the dead. Thermometers
　　　　　gossip in this world of flesh. Just miles from
this rented perch must be a farm of mud, a god's
　　　　　blood. A passport, of course, is no bandage.

2.

I'm off-course, wandering about this island
　　　　　despite the jet-lag, shyness, hangover, fear
of—what? Liza Minnelli calls her pet
　　　　　demon *Slick*. I like it here, champagne breaking
the fast. I feel brave like when my lost
　　　　　lesbian friend, Karmann Ghia—sí, like
the car—tried one night to call the actor
　　　　　Richard Harris who was in Bermuda.
She only got nervous when the operator
　　　　　started to sing: "We've got a ringdown.
A ringdown. We've got a ringdown." But
　　　　　no go, Joe. No one home. Back to the flack.
Tours of statue gardens, hardening art.

Incredible angels with unholy genitals
spread opaque wings across the pale sun.
                    Uncircumcised workers in stone soak up
our breaths. Galleries feature cameras
                    as portholes on long ships. Women in
sexy silk dresses of accents ask for
                    directions to mind museums. Room
service softens the harsh exhaustion: it's
                    Glenn's birthday! More wine! I tip with last year's
unused condoms! It's like my dream! We're on
                    the porch. And Auden is dead. I can't tell
the bay from the neighboring music
                    building's roof. God, Jesus Christ—why don't I
ever say Buddha?—Jimmy Smits is on
                    the TV, even here? Back to the view:
a volcano cools its toes across the way,
                    ocean blue as a mule's balls bearing
the coffee by which the civilized world
                    wakes up, or the cocaine it uses to
fuel its revolution against the actual.
                    I dress up like some Maine lumberjack
and rush to empty beaches to write home.
                    Water carries the weight of light, sweet wind and
man's puny ships. This isn't what I
                    say, though, to the German submarine sailors
that disembark while I search for a photo
                    opportunity: small poet at large.
To feel this young is to know I'm aging.
                    The Age of Anxiety has been milked by
Hollywood. Airplanes, from some myth, circle
                    the hotel—indiscreet dragons dragging
the Apocalypse to our eyes. Lovers
                    that have been mine, mostly as wonderful

false gods, wake up in my headache, stretch, kiss
        the air. *The hair of which dog?* Strange to be
so simple: a mumbling existentialist
        until the coffee that clicks, locks in; Buddha,
I'm a consumer after all. Place *is* a big meal.

    3.

A few submariners are in this café
        and they smile as if allegories
successful at escaping Dante.
        Clouds in the windows, a blinking ocean.
Danish is spoken here, a sweet language;
        is it what's spoken in Atlantis? I said
nothing to a friend whose lover died of
        AIDS in Manhattan, an island of *is*
becoming *was*. He told me this folk song
        in a flat voice, geography of grief:
A soft snowstorm seals the funeral home
        until the world looks like the eyeballs of
a man who stared at the wrong eclipse.
        Months later, drinks at Dancing Joe's, *and there's*
an architect who loves Bauhaus and rings.
        At first it's depressing to become
erotic inside a motel of nailed-down
        furniture, off-white towels, and a broken
ice machine. Then it's an adventure,
        a diary of sweat, stupid human tricks.
A shower makes one's body feel new. How old
        thoughts take over: do I have any talents?
I won't mourn all the time I've time. Nothing
        can be a sign of respect, sometimes.
This was a friend who'd never fly across
        an ocean to an island that is like some

period mark without a sentence; I'm
                not especially brave. Stubborn, perhaps, yes.
Next tour: a small house for world leaders
                in which to sell themselves to each other.
Everything here is part of my tour: even
                the public toilet with its cameras manned
by a snoring uniformed moralist! Of
                course there's graffiti near the arctic: *Free
Oliver North! Fuck Ken and not Barbie!*
                Mambo is fun! Clark Gable is Gone With
The Wind! *Viking love!* Menus offer me:
                *Polar fish soup, puffin snacks, bread with scallops
and Sicilian garlic, Eric the Red*
                chicken, red-necked beer and *restless vodka.*
And there are titles to paintings found in banks,
                cinemas, bakeries: *The Soul and His
Codpiece, Nordic Nun, Whole Whale, Thor's Rent
                Party, White Nights Linen.* These poems are
poems for books never to be written, books that
                might be burned in this age of computer fever.
Thinking turns any landscape into
                a letter from a future lover in the horizon.

        4.

How can this arctic rain be rain
                and not snow? It's transparent like under-
clothes worn by constellations. It's a law
                on this land: cars must always wear
the tiara of headlights. "Pale—Ljos—Hell"
                reads the costly beer bottle. Rest at last.
Even the brackish bar mirror takes a long
                breath. So what was real today? Blonds of
both sexes (three sexes?) compare blondnesses
                under a lightbulb. I think of Emerson's

102

transparent eyeball; was it attached to
　　　　　　a transparent body? A vacation is
for not thinking, but time out: rain freezes
　　　　　　　in the planned trees. What a cold fire that
reigns this day. I take up last night's liquids:
　　　　　　melted ice, semen, sweat, beer. I take two
aspirins. Soon, it's snowing in my blood.
　　　　　　　Snow is silk for the poor. Imagine winged
silkworms in the air. Buddha's tongue in my
　　　　　　mouth is like ice skating with blind lovers.
In the hotel lobby, I wash off street dust
　　　　　　with happy hour—what a cynical
name. I'm a silver miner taking his
　　　　　　first bath in weeks, grateful to be opaque.
I somewhat understand the wonder that
　　　　　　Marco Polo must have felt having sex
in a new world with his old body.
　　　　　　　Time to prep for a new day, but first a look
at lobby paintings. In one, red women
　　　　　　walk fat cows which tilt their blue heads to
the devil's flute. A day's yellow is muted in
　　　　　　an anonymous landscape. A quick climb
hurries me to my familiar damnation.
　　　　　　　I've no children, no matchbooks and a pair
of gloves for a giant. Outside, winds sculpt
　　　　　　the moonlight into a plain skeleton.
Days later and we meet Helgi for laughter
　　　　　　at the restaurant *Argentina* where
no one is or speaks Spanish. The wine is
　　　　　　Italian and inspires us to take a taxi
to find a party somewhere, anywhere, now.
　　　　　　　Instead I leave my wallet in the noisy
back seat; it's quickly returned to the hotel
　　　　　　discreetly, as if I still have some secrets!

5.

David Byrne is in Reykjavik this weekend,
             wearing soldiers like cheap jewelry. More
fun to sit in a dark room with sons and
             daughters of warriors pretending to be in
The Village. Smoke and vodka, vodka and
             smoke. Opaque ghosts. Soon, room service asks
if my *guest* needs towels or an extra chocolate
             nest on my pillow. A rush of museums
next, impromptu walks through cemeteries
             older than America, and we can't forget:
humble geysers, humming bakeries, hung-
             over population polite in cafés
and hard luck stories overheard in mouths
             of angel statues trembling in naked
parks. Trees are immigrants here. Houses are
             of corrugated iron painted all the colors
of Satan's toes in Milton's *Paradise*
             Lost. Serpent, half-goat, former president,
shit-head—no matter, for myths make room for
             all our relatives. Helgi meets us at
a church as impressively barren as
             some Old Testament wives. There is no fossil
evidence of Auden's journey here.
             Why? It was only hundreds of civil
wars ago. Internet was science fiction
             and modernism seemed modern, which it
was long after the spent youth of good souls.
             Back to room 318 of Hotel Holt, I dream
of home, as if it or I have ever existed.

6.

A good sleep, a deep shower, a sweet coffee,
              only why is it so late in the century?
Tourists mistake me for a *native* and
              why not guide them to (*eitthva*
um skin) (something about the clouds) as
              Icelandic poet Sjon writes. He also insists:
: hn hefur minnka eng er me gtukort
              og get veri viss um a villast
(: it has shrunk but I have a street map
              and can be sure of getting lost).
In *False North's* men's room, we talk of poetry
              as if that's all there is (as it *should* be).
The trickle down effect seems to work for
              icicles. To misquote Auden: *is that*
yet another entrance to purgatory
              or your asshole? Amazing what one will
shield from one's familiars. And then the gift:
              I rent a birthday plane and pilot, only
we're canceled. After a hike, we're told: go
              to the aurora borealis' aerial bed!
Credit card enlightenment of coarse debts!
              The Polish pilot is so handsome that
it's obvious heaven loves him:
              so we're safe in the three-seater
flying into skies over icebergs
              and volcanoes. How odd to feel
so free even as Puerto Rico
              prepares to celebrate 100 years
under America's thumb. White
              the waves, white the rivers, white
are noon's teeth! The plane's shadow
              scurries on land, and I think of

near-death experiences in which
          souls rise from bandaged bodies.
How lovely to be human, but winged!
          What I feel is the opposite of
Auden: *The stars are dead;*
          the animals will not look.
From the air, plain Earth is a star
          that breathes blue rivers and
ripe mountains. And we are
          the curious animals looking out of
the cool cockpit, for seeing
          is the basis of all poems, visions
and the greatest of love stories.
          I love Iceland for it is new, not mine,
and without the sorrows of
          my Puerto Rico. Public geysers
replace palm trees, glowing lava fields
          replace rain forests, boisterous snow
replaces white sand. How powerful
          to be between land and sky,
sea and sky, sky and sky.
          The pilot is proud of his cargo
of poets and so when we fly
          over a waterfall, he dives towards
the beautiful abyss and I'm
          not too afraid: ours is the vantage
point once only possessed by
          opium eaters and mystics on beds
of nails. We pull up and it becomes
          clear that Iceland is an island on
the island of Earth in a floating cosmos.
          It's something I know, but now
I know it with my own eyes.

I want this flight to never end:
the beautiful pilot, my true lover and
                    I suspended between laws of
gravity and history; we laugh
                    at *nothing* and *everything*, elements
that are ripe at last for the plucking.
                    Holy the hunger and holy the feeding.
Not the holiness of my coloring
                    books with prophets and gutted sheep,
but this ache in my bones above
                    this barren island bursting with life.

After the Paintings of Giotto

Jacob Receives The Blessing Of The First Born

My father can't tell the differences between a goat and his hairy son.

I don't have to destroy him.

Isaac Rejects Esau

My father is sure I brought him food earlier today.

His bed is for dreaming.

Mine is for tiring myself out.

Joseph Is Sold By His Brethren

I'm without my coat; my brothers pour wine on my nakedness so I can shine in

the cold desert night.

Cup Found In Benjamin's Pack

I am the youngest.

I can make love longer to any woman or man than my brothers can.

Lovers in Egypt will crush the moon, pour its white blood in my mouth.

I have many mouths.

The Slaying Of Abel

The argument is done.

I have proven to myself that the human body returns to the earth.

And stays there.

Doctors Of The Church And Saints

We paint the night's long blinks black so that light gets trapped inside us,
    mirrors to stars.

Release is our enemies' knowledge of heaven; most currencies have been
    based on loss.

Way Of The Cross

One soldier thinks of having his soft feet washed.

Not everyone's gods need be all powerful.

Christ Among The Doctors

He has no facial hair and could be a Greek youth about to throw a javelin.

His halo is an expensively fragile parasol.

Mourning The Dead Christ

A veiled woman, a corpse, a mountain locked into one season, a mourner
    listening to a seashell,

a cloud weeping like some cuckolded alchemist.

A Fragment

... and Pale Ramón borrows
a stepladder from the moon
for a better view of his tropics.
Maps are not very good
suitcases for each named city
takes up too much room
in the going towards gone.
He must be somewhere
where breath is money.
Rum lends color to the ghosts
in these red rain forests.
See-through harvests of
harsh cemeteries thicken
so the view is useless.
He falls off the stepladder
but Pale Ramón lands on
a fat angel's back and is
hijacked to a ruined castle inside
mountains of cumulus clouds.
It is peopled by crows in leather
who demand he recite the history
of literate Heaven in rhyming
couplets or else be tried
and tied to a thunderbolt
(*but can an Earthling's verse
be a dress rehearsal for glory?*).
Thus, the corruption of
imagination is exposed
to him, but it waits for
Pale Ramón to expose himself
in return: bone wear, soul's skin.

He writes a sad story
on the guest body of a falling
star, just burning black ice.
The more he rhymes *luck*,
the more black feathers are
shoved into his mouths.
Just as our hero despairs,
Pale Ramón is grabbed by
his river of long hair.
It's Adrenaline, that under-
worshipped god! Like
translucent saints of sex toys,
they get the hell out
of there. Dante asks for
a postcard from Puerto Rico,
something with pink fruit
manhandled by green monkeys.
Pale Ramón is out of breath
in the depth of his talent,
but how opaque are his
opulent palms? This was
a dream within a dream, not
the first such experience
among numb homo sapiens.
Before going to work,
Pale Ramón eats an orange.
It's a love letter from
the absent sun, each seed
the history of the planet Earth.
Pale Ramón has an idea,
a plan for a winged city that. . . .

from | *Home Movies Of Narcissus*

2002

Some Faces

Wearing this shaving cream mask,
I work towards a shining.
Later, I tell you in the bar,
Tierra Nueva: "Every brother
to his beard of beer foam!"
Youth loves to say yes, *sí*, aha.

❧

I pass a mirror, look at myself:
nude in a large net of light.
A mustache would disguise me
but why bother for morning
always finds me, calls me by name.
Hijo, I call myself, son of the sun.

❧

My morning beard signifies
that something happened
to me last night: midnight?
love? what? no souvenirs?
I wear my father's face in
a city older than my heart.

Delicious Parable

Here we are at a convenience store
with one row of Puerto Rican
products and my Mother crosses
herself. Nothing has prices, but
we fill up baskets with yautia,
platanos, and other edible maps.
Mother rushes and grabs the baccalao,
dried codfish. Tasty skeleton of salt,
it's the gilled grail, Neptune's diary.
Mother acts as if we're both jewelers
as the clerk weighs our goods—for
they are good. How much a pound?
Expensive, pensively so, OK, *sí*.
We drive back through ghettos in
which children don't play. Or eat?
The poor no longer have children, Mami,
and she nods—not listening for she's
planning tomorrow's meal. I cry
later at home, for this food is
the only inheritance she can give me,
this meal with chance bones in it.

Dream Starring Andy Garcia

He walked naked into
the party, put his
head on my hard lap,
wept because he
didn't have a shadow.
Talk turned to Greek
statues. He asked why
his morning beard was
black while his pubic hair
was red. I pushed him
into the shower. He
pulled me in and I
also wept with him
at not having a God
in any of my images.
The party dragged us
back into its endless
singing of "Happy Birthday"
to the sun. I stayed
in this dream until
9:45 AM when a beer truck
on Temple Street blew
its horn. Happiness
is so easily stolen.

A Bolero, But Not For Dancing

> Cecilia sits in the darkening living room in Puerto Rico.
> Her brother's male lover has come to tell of Juan Angel's
> funeral. Cecilia talks to make the meeting important, an
> event to remember.

What I dislike about daylight is its
muscularity. What need to claim
everything, only to release it
at dusk, when man and woman need a
godparent? Do you notice how my
hands seem blue and yet I'm wearing no
sapphire nor do I play the piano?
I'm the last in my family to go
gray, but what talent lies in that claim?
I do fly—in dreams in which I'm not
in Santurce, but on Saturn, or in
a Venice not yet painted by a
Puerto Rican. Curiosity
may well prove to be a domestic art.
If you notice, I live alone although
so does the sun and moon, but then they
share the same sky, small purple spaces
in my eyes. My desires I've tamed
because of experience: Orion
never does grow naked, the Big
Dipper never solves anyone's thirst
on Earth. From inside my house, this planet
seems flat, a matter of walls to knock
down, or build doors into, or from which
to hang photos. That's Juan Angel
on the beach on the night of some Saint.
Lord Byron, perhaps. No, that's a joke.

Juan called me his Sor Juana and I
did cry. I was forbidden to read as a
young girl. Knowledge was too unstable
a dowry. My brother was beautiful.
But you've seen him. You may know that
better than I do. But still, the white trunks,
the moonlight, the white foam of a wave
bound to break against him, light from
some galaxy in the sky—Sirius,
perhaps—sí, Sirius howling
overhead. See how a glass frame turns my
Juan Angel into a classical ghost.
There are mirrors and there are masks,
and there are always masks in the mirror.
It's easy to misquote the dead, no?
Now: only there is no now. Rum at least
lies to one. You must have driven blindly
down backroads of the grief that brought you
to me. Do I disappoint you with
my plainness? I'm not a tourist site.
Once conversations threatened to pull this
house apart, nail by nail, plank by plank,
but then once Juan Angel was alive.
He chose never to visit me because
then he couldn't be an orphan.
He never realized that I became one
too. I bought a parrot. At his death,
my brother's, and not the parrot's, though both
are dead, I got dressed in my leather
coat—unusual in my Puerto Rico
but that's the point. I went to see
the mummified remains of the island's
Vatican-approved St. Pio who
had been young, once. What remains is

the idea of his form, under the
bandages, below the glass coffin that
makes the saint seem a snob. So I left
my fingerprints all over the church
and cried for Juan Angel en el Parque
de Campanas, near a jail, a different
kind of church. You and I share similar
desires, not that most human
desires are very different from
each other. Except for serial killers
and Buddhist priests, both groups prizing
nothingness, abstinence of pleasure.
At least my priests are in constant and
perhaps eternal pain. And not over
love. But lust. It's the force that helped the
Barbarians batter the doors of
Roman empires. But that's not why I
have deadbolts. No, I have many dead.
I sat under the ordinary eyes of pigeons
without any bread to offer them and
I thought about the prisoners—in
cells at the bottom of that cliff. Naked
before God. I imagined them as
sailors forced into the fortresses
of their solitary natures. My
hand reached out for their visibility.
I walked towards the jail and looked down.
One man looked up and grabbed his crotch.
For me, it was a seashell grabbed from
the Aegean, a collect call from Neptune,
a blue rose from Atlantis, an eel
to cook in my famous garlic sauce.
Then the poor young boy left the yard and
entered hell, only without a Dante.

Oh, I know literature. Juan Angel
read it to me aloud because
growing up there was no pornography.
One just acted it out. I caught a dark
taxi away from that park and went to
an American bar. But I didn't look or
drink like a fallen or falling woman.
I don't own a radio. I used to have many
records, a great name for the music
that accompanies us. To break a record. To
record thoughts. I have some left. My second
lover gave me this bolero. He
was an athlete. Your height, but I think, more
hung. I make you blush? Enjoy a rose,
when you can. Was Juan Angel beautiful
and aggressive? Those two traits don't always
go together. Consider dolphins.
Beautiful but so dependent on the skirts
of cruise ships that pass through the blue
purgatory of the tropical peace.
I know that you were his . . . friend. Have I
tired you out? Is that in my power?
I'm sure he would comfort you now only
he is the one lost in true time itself.
I keep on breathing. I've walked around this
house so many times that my steps are
maps. But I hurt you by calling him
by name. Your smile is either a dismissal
or an admission. In either case,
it proves you've listened to me. You know
what you know, but not what I know. That
will never be yours. Amusing oneself
after 40 becomes an art. Art becomes
less and less about male statues coming

to life and stepping into white, tight gift
underwear from the moon. It's about
playing one song over and over
again, and learning how to stop weeping.
It's about one goddamn song in your
goddamn mind and how it's goddamn new
with each goddamn hearing. Nothing is
ever in our control. It is time for you
to leave, while you can, while the ghosts
under the palm trees are busy eating
each other, while sharks jump from roof to
roof to see if stars are the real surface
of the sea, while a taxi can be found
to take you back into your grief,
a different monster than mine. The sad
part, my friend, is that you will return
to your photographs of Juan Angel
and I'll have this simple one: Juan Angel
as a merman, clasped not in Abraham's
bosom but Neptune's, or a dead sailor's,
or Hart Crane's perhaps. See how we mourn
two different men? We are almost allies.

Cecilia locks the door after Nestor and shuts off all the
lights of the house. She watches her visitor disappear
into the moonlight. She goes through her jewelry box
and finds nothing that seems right for the occasion
for dreaming.

The Ponce de León Poems

1. I, Ponce de León, Return to our World

. . . and the miracle of the sea still stirs
my stilled skull. New light bursts from
my dark solar plexus. I'm back *home*
to the land haloed by human breath.
Alive again, I'm wounded my old islands
now have skyscrapers instead of palm trees.
The statues to me are unsung and gray with
years shunned by shock-proof tourists.
My poor hysterical Hispañola is
unhusbanded without me; Puerto Rico
turns *pobre*. I'm their red-haired hurricane
returned to economies of false starts.
Has that far fountain been found yet?
Am I old alone? How crowded these islands.
Something shakes me, something like a bell.
I'm seized, but not by a seizure. History
was easy once: a wave of my young sword
as I rode waves towards the craved kingdom
of the Eye. It was all mine to claim.
Hunger is still all I know of forever.
I'm no one's souvenir—but God's.
But not yet. Anonymity is the worm
that eats body and soul long after
burial, a deep sleep in real space.
To be forgotten is a daily death.
The sea has taught my spirit how to leash
a volcano and ride it towards cold light.
I must find a poet to haunt, someone
to help me forever flee the footnote.

2. The Poet Rejects Ponce de León's Offer to be a Muse

Sorry, Señor de Sorrows,
but I'm not the poet who
will write you a winged
epic, so grow bald
in that hairy grave.
A rum fiesta
is down the red
street: sunset. I still
live here, my here.
And, no, I'm not your
pet cockatoo. Your
mad rule over
stolen land is
over, and as for myth:
no fountain, no
gain. Gracias for
the passé anger,
but the dead are
always generous
with useless gifts.
We are wealthy with
our plastic surgeons,
plastic flatwear,
plastic flamingoes,
plastic card calypsos.
Ponce, we've improvised
your unfound fountain.
Some other writer
must need you, amigo,
a CyberLowRider,
a CosmiVaquero,

any CatholicSka
(a monk in dreads).
Leave me, Señor.
Seduce someone else with
fame or infamy.
The age of the epic
is gone, Governor,
and statues are
now abstract, story-free.
—Well, one poem then,
a catered exorcism,
a bon voyage for old bones.
Then *adiós*, conqueror.

3. Promised Poem: Being Ponce De León

The nobles among the sailors
use handkerchiefs
on their bloody noses.
The common sailors
wash their faces in the sea.
Under a Catholic God,
Ponce de León sneezes in
private. His holy breath
strains the starving sails.
He drinks wine, red as
the ruby fields reported
in India's riverbeds.
He walks naked under
the man-in-the-moon's scowl,
asks the drowned "Which
God claims your clatter?"
To calm himself down, Ponce
demands a civilizing shave:
23 servants spy on him
through narrow doors.
They mock his balding head,
comment that it's shaped like
a bony fist and that roses
in new worlds decay like
those in gardens left behind.
More wine is brought.
Some spills onto maps,
future trails of blood.

4. I, Ponce de León, Protest the Age of the Lyric

This poet is a clumsy ventriloquist
and this is what he publishes,
the bastard. I've killed for much less.
Arroyo is an amateur
magician; where are the maffick rhymes?
Jewels without cuts are only stones;
stones without shine are the skulls of stars.
Any lyric is a terrible lie
(it's the law of that form). This is his
pathetic séance, a mere brief aside.
What's up and down with that? That poem?
As monument to me? That black eye?
This poet has a piñata for a heart.
Learn, hijito—the accent mark
over the hard word "León" is
a savage knife falling from Heaven.

5. Promised Poem, Second Attempt: The Young Ponce De León

VOICES:
Numbers. Numbers.

PONCE'S FATHER:
My son is from and part
of the first family in Spain to join
Queen Isabella's crusade to turn us
into a giant who feeds on blood.

A NEIGHBOR:
He is just one of twenty-one sins against
the Holy Ghost, songs of misspent semen.
Twenty-one lions loose in old Spain.
Twenty-one Spains before one lion?

VOICES:
Numbers. Numbers.

A SOLDIER:
He wars at the age of fourteen.
Other boys' fathers rot in this aged land.
He gives neither Heaven or Hell hostages.
Hero by denying the zero in his bones.

A NUN:
Zero is the number we stole from The
Sahara. It's heterotropic in
our excesses of spiritual censure.
Zero shares the egg's shape, eyeballs, balls.

VOICES:
Numbers. Numbers.

COLUMBUS:
Zero flowers in the new world, home to
birds and ghosts—interchangeable species.

PONCE'S MOTHER:
The three-in-one god's ten commandments seem
to limit Juan Ponce de León to
vices older than his age but this rage
is aged wine, Satan's own victualer.

VOICES:
Numbers. Numbers.

PONCE:
A sum summarizes a summons.
The whole always hides holes, whore
with greater belief in the unending
to come than have comet readers or court
eunuchs. I am my own meaning.

6. *I, Ponce de León, am not Jealous of El Cid*

Ahh, what do they teach you in those
English language prisons? If the moon
drops diamonds without remorse, why not you?
Pero tienes miedo, hijo. Such fear.
Arroyo, replace light's windows
with tapestries. Opacity
is the heavy city of Jerusalem
crowded with Crusaders spending
their curt blood. My words, your mouth:
an ancient trade route. Transformation
is just a braggart. The old is old.
A witch of San Terva said to put
rags of roses in my mouth when
I was born: hunger. Then chickens were
sacrificed, cleaned, cooked because of my red
hair; I was the sun's bastard, wearing
my mother's burning blood inside and out.
Then the Moor wars, then I was a cocksman.
I steered my promiscuity until I was
a mast in a new world: "Follow a mermaid,"
I said to the enslaved compass.
Then the salty empire of my labor.
Too much now, too much then. Ships can burn
on water, know that? Learn that fever is both
the message and the messenger.
Write me a defense that distracts from facts.
The fountain between my legs, poeta,
that was history, el futuro, *el futuro.*

7. *The Poet Shakes off Ponce de León's Hungry Ghost*

Morning wakes up wearing
the holy underwear of snow.
The ventriloquist's séance
last night was a bust. No ghost
from a nearby star joins me
for coffee from Thailand, land
my speech therapist insists
I don't pronounce as Thigh-Land.
Gold roses the size of baby fists
make me think of Florida when
it flowered before being forced
to wear weary Eden's figleaf.
X used to call our lovemaking
a ménage which sounds like
a Dutch Elm disease. That's what
you get, Héctor told me long ago,
for having an imagination.
I was young a few hairstyles ago.
I'm back to my instant breakfast
and notebooks rotting like apples.

8. *The Poet's Nightmare with Cameo by Ponce de León*

The terrible Taino shows me his
wounds, and I put my hand
in the one near his heart. Cold,
the black hole there, a cold
not of the tropics. I am
accused of praising Him,
Ponce de León, the cross's
claw, the blood lover.
Then a hailstorm of heads of
Christianized slaves,
and each one cries out: write
of us who are buried
without tombstones far from
our mourners. I weep
because salt is an honest
gift that is ours to give:
Heaven, see my beard of tears.
A black moon mocks me.

    Ponce de León Interrupts:
We all speak sorrow, son.
It's the language of history.

9. The Exhausted Poet

To be young forever
is one way to overthrow
any of the graying gods.
But research what?
Untranslated papers
mispronounce the lost moments
of a man, a ship, a fountain.
He died on a far Cuba,
paradise become a casket.
One spring, I went to the cathedral
named for him and strangers
asked me to be a godfather
to their red son. "The rain
has caused delays and we believe Satan
wants the soul of our heir."
Where is that child? Where am I?
Ponce is also the pouting name
of a city in Puerto Rico but
its beautiful and famous fire station
can't cool this fever. I map
a lover for I've fate lines to deny.
The bedsheets are blank sheets of paper.
Ponce's ghost is lost! At last!
Noon, your big yellow is simple,
a bee's brain. I'm naked,
no Sunday paper. We hold on
to Saturday, laughing
that my silly erection
is an 11th finger, one that
wants either a wedding ring
or flea collar. I'll write these
Ponce de León poems later,
when I'm old. Delirious,
the cat, wants out, out there.
The radio: *oh, baby, it's a wild
world.* Like God's mind?

10. I, Ponce de León, Declare War On Poets

You are all memorialists with
nothing to confess. Narcissus,
at least, had his eyes open, and
that damming pool was of *this* world.
As black-clad black holes, poets
steal breaths of days meant to be
misspent, miserable, mislaid.
And for what? To excuse their drinking?
I will now haunt a historian, kinder
fabulist. Arroyo, I kick you to the curb,
and take your hipped Ricky Martin with you.
Puertorriqueños, you have forgotten
that Old Spain is your Mother who
demands blood, those liquid rubies.
We bribed the Gods we could, killed
the others. Poetry should praise scars.

11. I, Ponce de León, Say Goodbye to Puerto Rico Again

My island is as theatrical as
any sleepwalker's house. Your biblical
dependency on a fisherman explains
the hooks in your mouth, mouths. Unzipped, you
are the sun's zealot. That remains true. Beds
with tourists are never an escape route;
you are the foreigner in your own nights.
Midnight is my confidante, ever since
I was killed by an arrow, that plush *pling*,
a singing rush to a horizontal view of
the hardening ancient sky. Funny, how
softness is the dream now. Mine no saint's death:
no hot pokers up any of my known ports,
no cannibal's communion, no drowning
in my enemy's blood as did gilled Samson.
You are my zipcoded heir, poor puppet.
Isla, forgive our Arroyo for his conquering
words and not worlds; poets can be used
to hide the bodies from historians and God.
Don't hurt through heroin, hype, or hoopla
of Santería souvenir shopping. Don't hurt.
Priests have sold you to allies; know that
enemies are the best of all anchors.
Island of slow *sangre*, let others starve
their hearts; enjoy another feast on a
black tablecloth with pink silk-stitched stars,
the colors of old wounds. Your rainforest
veils overfed cities. Airports return
the coffins of your tired corpses, for cash.
Why isn't spectacle ever a condemnation?

But, sí, voting Republican can only lead
to blonde grandchildren, and see what good
they have done me? Turn coconuts into
milk nurses. Nothing wrong with stealing silver
from mirrors, but nothing brave about it.
Colonize the moonlight. Be worthy of love.

12. *The Poet Dreams of A City Crowded With Singing Statues*

The young age in each
other's dramas. Birds in
dancing trees. The multi-
lingual are silent in
the arms of their desires.
The city receives runaways,
its economics based on
the harvest of thrown-away
names. Go-go dancers imitate
the sex aches of Praise, that
half-god without a purpose.
The aged are amazed by
what is whole. Open any
door and hurry into opulent
music. Murals give births
to smiling suns who don't
seem too homesick for
the tropics. Chaos theoreticians
grow rich and bald. The young
are replaced by the younger.
Where are my honest ghosts?
What is a son without a father?
Statues keep predicting the wrong past.
Ponce? de León? Juan?

Aching in Autumn

My dying cat is purring because
I'm home from a wedding reception

in which Christian women shook
their holy vessels after champagne.

Auden, you must be bored being dead.
My Anita Josefina looks out

of the black window into the black.
She will teach me to the very end:

In his home movies, Narcissus
is both the seen and the seer.

Write What You Know

But what do I know? I know Papi
worked in factories reigned by melodrama
(a sick day = the righteous anger of

waltzing bosses in *Kmart* suits). I know
the word "knowledge" has the words
"now" and "ledge." I know that

my parents dared to color the suburbs
with their shy children. I'm no longer shy.
"Chew garlic," Mami said just yesterday after

I was diagnosed with pneumonia (I can't yet
breathe in the America I so love.) I must write
about the time a museum guard yelled

at Papi: "the service entrance is over there."
Forgive me, Papi, for wanting to see dinosaurs.
(He's an aging man who abandoned me as an adult.)

Papi was silly, but he stopped dreaming
after citizen classes (but Puerto Ricans are
Americans I must still tell my frowning

scholarship geniuses.) I know that Uncle
Manolo who died in the green disgrace
of gangrene did want to teach me the 12-string

guitar but we visited less and less until
we were merely scars to each other, sad
genealogies. I know una tía became religious

decades after offering me a *Playboy* and
an eggtimer. I know another tía talks
to spirits between epilepsy carnivals.

She is sweet and tough, what the grave
yearns for when thinking of honey.
I know that in poetry workshops I've lied:

"I'm not autobiographical." *They* don't need
to know Mami ripped a real blouse while
screaming at Heaven as if eavesdropper

with a big diary. Papi's pornography was
disappointing because it wasn't imaginative.
I know I was judgmental, one way

to survive. I know that I miss feeding the camels
of the three wise men (forget the presents—
camels in Chicago!). I know my teacher in

elementary school told me she was *glad* that
someday I'd be raped in prison. I know that
I've masturbated towards fake passports.

I've always loved details as if they are
sharable coins. I know that some colleagues
treating me to one dinner were naive in thinking

I knew the Mexican waiters who cursed them
every time they smiled under the parachutes of
fragile mustaches. We were and weren't strangers.

Will I get an award for knowing Mami hid her silver
Jack Kennedy dollars in the bathroom? I know God
has plans for me but I rather do it myself, gracias.

I write without permission and no one knows how
often I'm rejected and when I do publish *they* smirk,
"Affirmative Action." My future is as an antique.

I know a man's morning beard can rub me raw
so that it feels that even sandpaper has a soul.
I know that I want to be known in my earned bed,

that it's worth it to be kept out of anthologies
because machos clone themselves without end.
My crotch has a mind of its own; I'm a double exile.

Sí, I know that none of this matters and yet
it hurts, it hurts. I know that once upon a time,
I used to be a brave little brown boy. The man I am

has memory losses that medicine can't help.
I know there are evil men trying to trade
new poems for old poems: newer, swifter,

correct models. I know that the writing
workshop is a minefield. I know that I cannot
stop writing, that the involuntary muscles

are in it for the long run. I know I must
write to scare myself. I know that my beloved
Hardy Boys may never recognize me

from other migrant workers while solving
The Mystery of the Lost Muchacho.
I'm waving to them: here I am, here I am.

Hombres, how many more clues do you need?

That Flag

The *Motel 6* clerk thinks I'm
Italian and complains to me
about Puerto Ricans and I
nod because she has the key
to the last cheap room in town.
I unpack and go for a ride
down Joe Peréz Road and watch
two white, shirtless men do drug deals.
One looks at me, laughs. What does
he see? This sexy thug has
a Confederate flag in his truck
window. He rubs himself again
and again and I watch the way
one is possessed by a wreck.
The deal done, the two men then
slap each other on the ass,
and ride dust storms back to town.
I sit there thinking the fuckers
are right, that they are big
handsome, that they are our
America's perfect heirs and
that I'm not-aging Puerto Rican
homosexual poet exiled
to a borrowed bed. I walk
past the clerk and sing "Buenas
noches" but it isn't one for I dream
of that flag, of a terrible army
of soldiers in uniforms of skin
sent to steal from me the head
of Joe Peréz. But I've hidden it
inside my own skull. It is safe.

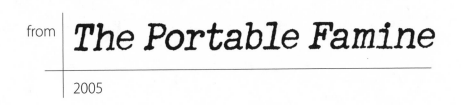

The Singer Enrique Iglesias As My Muse
In These Troubled Times

Enrique, you and I swim in a pool on
the Empire State Building's rooftop. How

far from sharks must we be? forever?
Clouds turn into steppingstones.

Suddenly, we're in Babylon and you
take off my gold cross, hide it in your

mouth. Questioned, we are stripped
and painted the red of Puerto Rican

roosters. Bees carry you to God. I limp
home where you somehow wait wearing

flesh again. We compare morning beards.
Music yields to the *yes* underneath breath.

We exchange shadows, glow without
greed and let winged goats eat the roof.

Details As Revelations

It's my turn to buy the condoms.
The cashier blushes at the possibilities
we've been conquering. I also buy

bleach, a toy mouse for the cat, underwear
for you to take off me. We don't talk
about a future. The street shines with

mannequins in rhinestone. We walk
as if just friends. We stop at *Big Books*
and there is a sale on literary critics,

half-off. You know before foreplay
there is foreplay, the mind's turn to
ride shotgun. We end up at *Pearlia's*

for a happy hour populated by extras
from *Dracula: The Musical.* Off-off-off
Broadway isn't a real neighborhood.

CNN is overthrown by the jukebox.
We compare passports, gods, and shoe
deals. You want to be seen. With me!

I'm not sure why. We talk about nothing
as if it's everything. We order a last round
to hurry back to my room, to a happiness.

Mayberry, RFD

Not even one illegal Mexican
in the body shop? No Guatemalan
maid at One Hour Motel? Not

a Puertorriqueña owning
a Tex-Mex restaurant? How
white *is* white? Poor Opie,

taught to fear jalapeños.
Even in imaginary America,
America has to be imagined.

Saturday Night In San Juan With The Right Sailors

I'm younger than the calendar. We like this
floating on bar stools, mermen amazed by
our miraculous sea legs. Apocalypse has

nothing to offer, upstaged as it is by this
jukebox playing Shakira—as if noise staves off
dawn. They rub against me for I'm the shore

of their shore leaves. It's just before the heat
leads to choices, and we like this competition
between beers and our fate lines, the risks.

Almost A Revolution For Two In Bed

You're still the island of the holy
palm tree. What can I offer to the man
married first to God, and then soon to
the wrong rib? Here, it's shining outside,
a spy stirred by the colors between us.
The sea is never rhetorical and asks
about your nakedness, that theater.

❧

You weep because your clothes
drag you back to vows. I will not
comfort you, not be another goddamn
mosquito net for Adam's innocents,
not shave this dawn's whiskers of
whispers. Coconuts look the balls
of angels refusing perfection.

❧

You leave. I stay. We fall off
the bed, this time as ghosts.
Winds steal words from books.
In the mirror, I see verbs,
read Arenas' Arenas, discover
love letters inside my irises,
rediscover Homer's honesty:
we return to our leavings.

Water Finds Its Own Level Even In A Desert:

Palm Springs Poems

Years after leaving Utah, I'm still
leaving it. This private playground
offers proof to me that I'm no longer that
Mormon elder too young for himself.
Clothing optional doesn't mean soulless.
It's an adolescent version of owed
adulthood: palm trees with nude tourists
not thinking about God, a guest book
for comments ("my first kiss was
in Room 14"— my room for the week!).
St. Reinaldo Arenas, pleasure isn't
a good widower. More comments: "rain is
coming. Hopefully I well [sic] be soon."
I'm explicit, and like the stewardess
said earlier, easily: "shift happens."
It's amazing that humans love
other human love. On my bed is
a safe-sex kit, bar guides, sun block.
But I came to be seen in this obscene
California light. I sit by the pool, unfazed
by the fact that I'll never be a martyr.

❧

Reading my beloved Shelley, I
envy Lord Byron. Others around
the unblinking pool read of
murder and sex in throwaway
editions of the libido. To be of
this Earth. I'm being stared at:
are secrets showing? showing off?
Naked men are rarely manifestos.

Earlier, I saw a wild rooster in
an empty lot. Its plain colors
were mistranslations of Psalms.
My shadow is unshod, unsure.

The erotic publishes books that
use vanishing ink, books of breaths.
Let's go inside, neglect noon, for
we are right: everyone is mysterious.
Without pretense, this hotel room's
painting insists the naked laborer
is more important than St. Mark's.
Our own nakedness is one way to talk.
It's true that we gloat about what we
can steal from God. I'm in unholy
Palm Springs where my body has yet
to embrace a man without a gold cross.

❧

Adam's free-range crotch
survives only as a dense book
of dream interpretations:
palm trees in snow means tragic love;
a magic wand means a dark forest:
a city of aching bridges means
some myth is starving to death.
But what of these magnets in skin
lent by sunlight? They—we—
wear warmth in the moonlight,
our solar plexuses as secret suns.
A pool waits to borrow form.
Immanence is always seductive,
the Now as an explicitness. The desert
knows how to flower. Strangers
kiss us back, men freed of contexts.
We're not just ideas—not when we're
clumsy, when offerings are deliberate.

The Visitor

el pan azul de cada día
[each day's blue bread]
—Pablo Neruda, "The thrush warbled, pure bird."

You're dead, but your skies are not.
This Ohio storm makes me think of your
blackening Chilean horizons. What use

is your name now in the not-now,
not-here? Neruda. Ne. Ruda. Neru.
Da. It was a wonderful mask, no?

Pablito, there is a spider in my spinning
bedroom with blind rubies for eyes.
Is this a message from you? Dawn is

still painful, old amigo, and pain is
always a vague ghost nostalgic for
the blue bread that we eat to forget

our missing talent for love. The dead
have mud for skies, ¿no? Imagine, poet,
we can incorporate, sell shares in ourselves!

Sí, the world is still extraliterary. Are there
bakers in the afterlife? Poetry asks for you
by name, the one finally yours. Stop grinning.

The Burrito King Of Toledo, Ohio

for Maggie Anderson

My father worked in a factory
that had no windows. For years,
he sweated in the bottom of this
abstract ship, never seeing ports,

but always returning to our bills.
He hasn't worked at summing his
life, hasn't worked at titling
his imaginary Selected Poems

as I have: *Midwest Matador*,
or perhaps, *This Country of
Scarecrows*. I'm addicted to dawn,
to light, to vision. I always carry

a notebook with me should anyone
say, this isn't work, this isn't work.
Look, I'll say, I've pages of notes,
most of which will become nothing,

won't become money in the bank.
Perhaps in years, when my poem,
The Burrito King of Toledo, Ohio, is
published, labor will be honored:

mine, my father's. Many days I've
walked into a sea of grass, just
outside of a factory, and have watched
men vanish during shift changes.

It's Dante, imported, more efficient
(no morally exact rhymes to "I'm
fucking tired."). I get to go home with
clean hands, but this worker's shadows

dirty many pages. I've arrived here,
Papi, to this inland embassy, for us,
for when there was an us. Now,
you and your eye-seeing dog try not

to get lost in your Puerto Rico, while
I select new short cuts to get home fast.
The tombstone only offers us breathing
space on its permanent hyphen, island

floating between heaven and hell. It's time
to go through the Taco Bell drive-through,
car blasting Jennifer Lopez's *Reel Life*.
I give my notebook, and myself, a day off.

Imitations Of Bruce Springsteen

for my lost compañeros

I drove like Magellan
on reds in a maze of ripe
curves, my darkness
more constant than sunrise
and less of an expensive
date. Driving nowhere and
praying to God we'd never
arrive there, Jorge often
rolled down his window
to scream: *There is no Utah.*
Springsteen's "Badlands"
spurred us to own *something.*
We sang along off-key while
throwing our clothes out of
the fast car as if corn silk.

❧

Back to lost Provo, I marvel that
the Saints sleep with their doors
unlocked. The stoned and stunned
still cruise Main Street, just chasing
their own tales. This is my America,
at last, the Mother Lode (*con su
permiso, Señora*), the Big Enchilada.
We race in the street while blasting
"Racing In The Streets." Postmodern
car locos. At secret parties, we are
truths: cowboys seeking straw beds
in which to yield to invisible forces.

The newness of my body over yours
isn't yet a spiritual crisis. As Deidre
points out, drama is dangerous. Ask
the angel Moroni: "Nothing sadder than
empires without forwarding addresses."
What's left of the Spanish conquest of
the Rockies is *True Taco*, where the illegal
and the immoral sit next to each other
after the Utah bars have squeezed sweat
from us, we who may never know mermen.
Back into the temple of the truck, we drive
without fear on confluent canyon roads.
We loop "Darkness On The Edge of Town"
while burning for the miracle of a city,
ending up far from God and nearer
to motels with morticians on call. Sí,
pull me to you, but understand: to be
stoned alive just takes found stones.

Mortals:
London Poems

How dirty London is this grainy
Ash Wednesday. Papers and
flyers twist and crash while we
with ripping maps seek roads toward
house-broken and poker-faced
palaces. Facets of colonialism
have been turned respectable as
fat museums, harmless graves.
Romanian beggars show undraped
photos of their saintless babies.
Locals clad in black walk with
cell phones, soloists stuck in choirs.
I must choose now: a near pub or
the artistic Apocalypse exhibit?
Cold ale is for us joyful mortals.
In the comradery of the dark bar,
I'm losing London while being foolish:
Angel Clare isn't waiting for me still.

❧

What a cliché—a prostitute
in Soho. I ask, "haven't you
ever read Marx?" Shops offer
sex toys without leashes, leather
loincloths, and winks. Back to
my tiny hotel room, I read
frank Frank O'Hara's *Lunch
Poems* (it's where I hide my
Traveler's Checks). He sings
in "Memoir of Sergei O…":

You are ruining your awful
country and me / it's not new.
Reading is labor not about pay.
Earlier a stranger sized me up
and handed a card: "you look
like trouble, a dash of *something*."
Invited to a Spice Girl bash,
3 A.M. seems an impossible
starting line. Heaven, the club,
will thrive without my freed
verse. My restlessness isn't
about events or the eventual.
The shower stall is a coffin,
a space shuttle, a fake bullet,
a generic forgiveness of dirt.
I put on my public uniform
of cologne and ignorant jeans.
I'm Pip of *Great Expectations*
pub crawling. My body wants
to be someone else's history.
I'm a new world with condoms,
sideburns and prayers to waste.
This dark city loves its broken heart.

❧

William Blake, the gods punished you
with talent. Poet and painter,
your words hide words in which
a snake coils about a naked
prophet; Abel's body is found;
Christ is a swordsman without
a funny bone. Alpha and Omega
want to own everything, again.

Your "The Ghost of a Flea" predicts
the modern human, Prometheus
forced to go Vegas. A crowd
gathers to see if you'll blink.
You don't. A man with cropped
hair cruises me, but I'm here for
the dark art on the white walls.
Who will box our ears these days?
The meek are incorporated and
the Tiger won't be our messiah
without a golden parachute.
Blake, I say later at The Goose
and Granite, poet, Earth is still
plagued with ghosts and fleas.
I buy rounds but fail to turn us
into illuminated manuscripts.

❧

I'm a tourist without a camera.
Forget St. Paul's and its tired frown,
better this handsome tourist—I must
interrupt this poem but a dwarf just
collapsed! Strangers laugh!—this
handsome tourist who rivals stern
revelations. Let the vague ghosts in
the cathedral pose for 3rd world cameras.
Architecture attempts to own Truth,
get fat on its franchises, prey on the praying.
I've a much closer prophecy. He sees me
seeing him and winks. T.S. Eliot, we
like being human. I ask the stranger his
gray Tuesday's Christian name: *Adam.*
Of course, perfect. An act of God.

Strolling through genteel
gardens contested by dogs,
abandoned suffragettes and
activists with one-cell cell phones.
It's not America I miss, but
Puerto Rico. A passing truck
still blasts Ricky Martin's "Living
La Vida Loca." I'm returned to
Bloomsbury where they sell
Virginia Woolf burgers.
I'm dizzy (do men faint?) but change
clothes to meet midnight halfway.
Ricky Martin's crotch is a puzzle
to the purists. Let him enjoy
youth, peddle his aspirations.
It's an age in which brown might not
be a bastard on the color wheel.
Ricky is a bottom on top, trickster
with copyrighted codpiece. Sure, I
wouldn't kick him out of my hammock.
(Empires are ideas first.) Drunk in
Soho, I buy leather pants that cut
my visit down by a week. Still, it's
good to act like my old shoes' I.Q.
and to be younger than my wisdom.
Dawn: a faceless stone mummy blocks
my path. Superstitions trump
my advanced degrees. I retreat,
stumble into the bored Virgin Records'
Superstore and here is Ricky
singing again! Amigo, we're sad
ambassadors from a country
that doesn't exist. Will it ever?

Letter To A Soldier In Iraq

We barbecue in your honor, the marinated
as miracles. Your ex is collecting angels,
one way to crowd the mind. My goatee

is gone, leaving just the ghost of my face
in bar mirrors blackening from smoke
without an exit door. Any visits from

Jesus? Buddha? Route 9 is closed so we'll
have to use Shore Road when we hunt new
naked midnights. Prayers are becoming

censors. Been thinking about Judas, how he
was just a bad poker player. Let's envy
rock singers who party in just underwear.

Scholarships are still birthing Republicans.
In your last letter, Iraq seemed a ruin
built on runes. Who wants to die when

there are sins yet to tame? We are polled
as if we can pollinate policies. Imagine:
you with a gun, abs, absolutes. Do you

miss fortune cookies? our illegal swims?
You might die for all this glitter on TV,
celebrities playing bed tag. Please, come

back. Politics is when adrenalin makes one
grab another man, hold him for his truth.
Write when you can, when you can tell.

Book Signings

A handsome man buys my book, asks me to read
his poetry sequence about Pablo Casals that's in
a suitcase in a bus station nest. It's a time when
anyone can be an enemy combatant because
of bad luck—ah, no. I sign my name over and
over again, as if I'm in a killer bee spelling bee.
Why do these hieroglyphics matter to strangers?
I have yet to heal my mirror, much less theirs.

❧

One reader is a chiseled Christian, a library in
tight jeans. Another is Zoracaster just flirting at
a taco stand; he's a new poem waiting a poet.
My exhaustion feels like jet lag without the journey.
I carry a leather notebook—in case of? A poem or
any motorcycle rides out of the mysteries of my myself.
I'm mistaken for Robert Downey, Jr.—in a mug shot?
I sign my books, stop owning them, and mourn later.

❧

I sign, but think of Sandburg's tall Chicago, Hughes' Harlem
of shiny shoes, Arenas' vanishing Cuba, Ritsos' Greece of
erotic ghosts, Hemingway's pubic Paris, Dos Passes' scared
USA, Armchair's unedited Jerusalem, our O'Hara's NY of
"sun-like" Puertorriqueños, Paz's silent Tijuana, Gasoline's Rome
of stigmata feasts, Auden's horsed Iceland, Sherwood's Berlin
in a bad blonde wig, Haney's mud-fed paradise, Calvin's
floating Italy and Arroyo's—will any place actually be mine?

Leaving Again

There is no room in my suitcases
for statues from my parents' faith
or a horizon kept from despair
by the movement of seagull mobs.

No, I return home empty-handed,
rehearsal for that slow ride across
the unintelligible River Styx
where even the human body

is left behind to root in the rot.
Sometimes, the sea visits me as if
smuggled, as if an apocryphal
book to memorize to keep it safe

in a library that cannot be torched.
The consuming sea brings no news
of what remains afloat on it.
It has no interest in any kind

of metaphysical drowning and
it withdraws without warning
until I wake up, until I sink in
foreign moonlight even though

logically there is only one moon
that hovers over us like a fate
older than our cosmologies.
Mystery has kingdoms without end.

Most attempts at globosity
turn consciousness into commerce.
The regional becomes summary:
the iconic seashell bracelet,

the wayward voodoo lottery god,
the Bacardi rum bottles that
are sold as the sun's alchemists.
My souvenirs? The portable famine,

the dying compass, the absent tide.
After I unpack from my journeys
I get drunk from the weightlessness.
Let fewer commercial maps be drawn

with blank spaces once thought to be lairs
of monsters and non-Christian gods.
Each newer journey dazzles as if a dumb
magnet. I'm often puzzled that what

can be read slowly on a spinning globe
remains abstract, even if visited with
my contemporary flesh and desires.
Writers and readers, why has Sisyphus

stolen the limelight? Again, I unpack
condoms, continents, continuances.
Soon, I repack them. My Caribbean
may never have been mine at all.

I watch strangers changing the time on
watches and I wonder what is unwatched.
Questions have always been feasts.
Leaving again, arrival seems an arrogance.

Ghost Island: New Poems

Fall And All (November 2005)

William Carlos Williams, much is new since
your last visit: wars, my iPod, Latinos voting
Republican, J-Lo married—a Boriqueño!
Perhaps Pluto might be demoted as a planet,
but it now evokes Mickey Mouse's dog and
not the Lord of the Underworld. In this hospital,
I miss home cooking—pasteles with Spanish
rice and red beans—and do the dead hunger
for food and not just significance? Slow
down, por favor. It hurts to teach your
work, forgive me, but I can't hear more
complaints that you aren't really modern,
won't read one more paper on wheelbarrows.
Red, I once yelled, red like the sun's heart.

 &

My male lovers feel safe just in the city
with its taxis and taxonomies. The doctor
repeats that I was two days away from dying,
but I heard *too dazed*. Hombre, I thought of
Uncle Rachel and his AIDS and said, *too
dazzled*. Carlos, I want you as my physician,
me riding shotgun on a que será será road
trip, but time for my urine sample so let's
make an illegal U-Turn in radiology. How
long since anything glowing has awed me?
One lover in Puerto Rico, but he was hard
work for a few poems. Can you smuggle
my new work out? Perhaps the vultures
will follow you. The joke will be on them.

Blood transfusions. My assigned internist:
Dr. Blood. Real life is so interesting and why
I think séances are for those without any
imagination. I think of Captain Blood.
No one uses "swashbuckler" in everyday
conversation or in personal ads. My lover
asks, "do you hear the strangers in your
new blood?" Blood oranges. Blood simple.
The drop of the drip. A rip tide in slow mo.

The nurse confirms that I still have vitals.
My robe is a poor figleaf. My ass looks like
a globe seen in a mirror full of fingerprints,
Satan's paperweight. Dr. Blood won't sign
a release until I've no fever. Blood's fire.
I eat ice. Now my temperature is too low.
Morgue humor. I'm bored. I'm not allowed
to sleep or to sneak in a party like Bob Fosse's
All That Jazz. My new blood may drown me,
but I'm going home now. I'm released, real
again. Carlito, push my wheelchair to the exit.
I'll send you news of the world that we both love.

Aging Protagonist (2006 Version)

I call God collect and I'm answered
with a dream: *a dead hummingbird*
nests in my mailbox. I wake to the song

of a bee's parts struggling against
each other for flight. A feverish
light burns into my notebook of

dreams. Once, meaning mattered,
lingered. Even as a boy, new days
would age under my many demands.

I drink coffee on the front porch (very
Elephant Walk) and taste air from Canada.
A packed suitcase will not be my crypt.

I've keys, keyholes, and keystrokes.
There are still many rooms to fill up
with tropical flowers and my low voice.

Ghost Island

Puerto Rico, I wake up so far
from your bed. There are no
roosters in my quilt-patterned
pale northern neighborhood.
Isla, you are supposed to float
on the sea and not in human
minds, yet here you are with
the need to smell my body as if
I've been with a rival paradise.

❧

Maumee Bay, Toledo, Ohio

Seagulls sit on their shadows.
Waves reach out to touch
everything that they're not.

My notebook would be wings,
fins or both. I look for patterns
in wildflower wanderlust

as if tides can reach this far
inland. Light touches everything,
keeps nothing. I'm a bicyclist

who's too aware of near cycles.
I've replaced the Caribbean
with this lake. Look! A deer,

but I scare away my best witness
to this new life far from an island
shaped by tides full of sharks.

The drowned won't stop circling
my island. Their eyes are not
perfect pearls; their hearts are not

secret volcanoes. There is no path
for them to join us on brief beaches
where we light illogical fires to keep

the living drunk and singing aloud.
Retroflexed driftwood disturbs with
its plainness, purity. Sometimes

shells offer words, but the noise
of this nilpotent world overwhelms
the fragile gates of the inner ear.

The Puerto Rico inside Puerto Rico,
my shadow's shadow. Think of how

a skull is generic even while wearing
the grace of astonishment—and yet

when it's the skull of one's beloved,
the specific yields to the spiritual.

The man outside of my male self,
call and response with genitalia.

The map of skin and the skin of maps.
Sailor as port, the unimportant nights

on shore. Drowning inside arms
while flying, while looking down at

our upscale Eden. Bring your own
serpent and apples, naked light

provided by geography, grace.
Sharing razors, the shine of godliness

far from commandments. Body hair
speaks *tide* and means *fire*. Adiós

brief pause, sunset's eternity.
The nakedness after the nakedness.

Island inside island, the sea inside
tears, tears lost inside the sea.

He is in San Juan writing letters
to his dead. His books are safe

from shark attacks, his shadow
laughing at tarantulas biting it

over and over again. The sublime
has tougher skin than what it's

been credited for. Broken glass fails
to distract from Caribbean stars.

It feels good to be alone, eating
cold red soup so close to midnight.

He has seen the cemeteries built
above sea level. Death is explicit here,

the continuous rotting that feeds
rain forests. This city won't wink

back, its lights going out one by one.
He's drowning in the beautiful dark.

～

Someone has forgotten a photo in
the library's *Collected Poems of Yeats*:
an eyeless man holds a red baby in

a bar and two other drunks conspiring
against dawn under Scotch's yellow tree.
The date: 9-5-92. The back of the photo:

Made in Germany and *Mystic Color*. Ireland
and Puerto Rico shake hands. Clues of
the past are too sentimental viewed from

my graying window. It was just snowing,
stout flakes on Fat Tuesday. Shut-ins
complain to the radio station: *too much*

Vivaldi. We all do need color and mysticism
to understand what is understandable.
The apocalypse, says a Boriqueño poet,

will wear the tropics' spectrum and waste it.
Soon, in dead weight coats and gloves
we laugh at our lovely addiction to the sun.

I've been changed by years of eating
apples and not mangoes. Alchemy

has been the basis of most victories:
soldiers into statues; barbarians into

brother-in-laws; gods into tax breaks.
There are more heir apparents than

inheritances, more lovers than love.
Many of us ache for this ghost island,

this period mark not yet solidified,
this lucent stone stolen from the sea.

Melting Cathedral

for Juanita Serrano de Jesus,
my grandmother and sanctuary gone

Shut your tiny mouth, Priest
for you didn't know her and
it's still too soon, too soon.

She loved party dresses (loves?)
and wanted to be buried in pink
(and she is in her pink coffin).
for Abuela was a salsa queen.

It's too hot in the cathedral but
not because of lit candles
in a sterile summer and
not because of our black clothes.

We're swaying so not to faint
while Abuela is read her
Miranda Rights for the grave
by gay men married to Christ who
make us sing and kneel, sing and kneel.

Her glory was not that
she left behind statistics—
"she was 95 so it was her time
and no one is sure how
many great-grandchildren she had."

I know she liked to laugh just
to expand a room and
she'd call me even though

I was evil non grata for
sleeping with men, a few of
them stolen from Christ's flock.
Genet knew funeral rites,
but these are not for thinking.

Only five mourners rush forward
for communion, five hungry
for the epiphany on a day
of ashes, ashes, ashes.
Ashes in my eyes,
my mouth, up my ass,
in my heart, and
all other openings to this world.

She and I talked each
Valentine's Day—not about hearts,
but about the arrows.
Cupid as the assassin.
It was a black anniversary.
She and I kept Uncle Rachel
from vanishing off the Earth:
"a ghost is better than nothing."

She gave me a benediction
at the start of all talks
and weighed my skull with
"The Virgin and all the Saints of Heaven
be with you."
                    "Pero, Abuela,
all of them? Where will they sleep
in my tiny apartment?"
                    "Junito,
you are like me, you are like me."

But I'm alive—for now
in this melting cathedral.
Electric fans spin and overfeed
the fires within me.

Would I pick up any of
the priests at a gay bar?
Costume change is change.
Abuela understood desire's
curiosity, that not asking
questions is a slow death.

She knew me before I knew English.
She gave me Christmas presents
after not eating well for weeks.
She lost her English at the nursing home
and forgot so many souls, but
knew me when I'd show up
after going AWOL from conferences
about poetry & community.
"Junito, why are you so skinny?"
Some visits, I was too fat.

Then one priest sings "Ave Maria" and
I cry.
Not for the Virgin. Not for Abuela.
Not for my mother. Not for myself.
"Ave Maria" was her favorite song:
"It makes me feel like maybe one day
I'll have wings too."

There are statues of angels with wings
here who have scraped faces.

The pallbearers stand up,
but I'm not one of them for
I would never carry her into a cathedral.
She belongs to me and not God
who should be in Iraq healing
the capitalists' collateral damage.

Pallbearers with blue gloves.
Pallbearers sharing my blood.
Pallbearers in shoes shined hours ago.
Pallbearers with appalling humility.
Pallbearers growing gray.
Pallbearers with whom I've shared drinks.
Pallbearers like soldiers unsure
of the name of their latest wars.

She said, "Junito, your Uncle Rachel
told me he talked to you before he died.
Don't tell me what he said.
That's the only thing he could leave you.
It's just yours."

The coffin heads to the exit door,
feet first.

The priests look at each
other, nod, and look at us.
I stare at them and one grins at me.
He knows I know that he knows
I know about him and he knows
about me and the almost naked
statues of saints that don't blush.
No one else notices.

We all follow the coffin,
pink island sinking back into the sea.
Stepping outside,
the sunlight burns my eyes but
it's not the sun of my tropics.

I want to blast salsa in the cathedral.
I want it to be heard in the Vatican
with its new Hitler-Youth old man.
I want it to awaken her from death.
No, she's being hurried into the hearse.

We're late, yells the driver to my Uncle who
says, Take your time.
This is our funeral,
our funeral,
ours.

Guardian Spirit

1. Listening to The Supremes' *Greatest Hits* as America Weeps for Ronald Reagan

The unashamed always get the cover photos,
their mob of mourners in photogenic poses.

I need black women to sing to me, their voices
saying what the lyrics cannot—not yet, but when?

Come on Miss Diana, hurry that love, let's be
together now. My drag queen uncle died while

Reagan was learning how to spell A-I-D-S. Where
is Uncle Rachel's statue, the national mourning?

2. Uncle Rachel Visits Me Again In Austin

Look, hijo, racks of hunks
on postcards, male mail.
Who isn't uprooted? Old news.
You're running out of costume
changes. That's badass sushi
karma, pilgrim, so go out tonight.
Buy me any flagrant wine and
pour it into the nearest river.
Eventually it'll flood my soul.
Write of your cowboy conquests,
gravity's athletes without souls,
sailors in love with scarecrows.
Those are the postcards I want.

False West:

Hollywood Poems

I go often to Hollywood, "unreal city,"
because I ripen in its singing streets,
grow a goatee because of angst's latest look
(masks are de rigueur here), and
seek asylum. But I'm not on the A list.
Only the sun is unscripted in L.A. and
it's best to put destiny on the back burner
and be typecasted until the big break
offers salvation. If the rigorously beautiful
can survive their free will, so can I.

❧

Hollywood isn't Eliot's dark woods,
Dante's holy woods, or Harriet Tubman's good woods,
or the black forests of Neruda's last breaths.
It's more Little Red Ridinghood's toothy woods.
Hauntings in modernized heads
require budgets and no slow hallowing.
For mountains here, gelded bodybuilders.
Instead of rivers, martini actresses' best tears.
As the sea's stunt doubles, mulling pool boys.
Replacing hills, a skyline of trained breasts.
Wolves are proving that they'll inherit the Earth.
Corporal corporations copyright the sky.
(Stars require exquisite heights in order to fall.)

❧

I'm asked, "Who will play you in the movie
based on your life?" The wrong answer is
myself. After enough psychic wine and
mea culpa footsies with Fate, I want those
blue screen nights that launch dancers

from chimneys, reveal orchestras with orchids
in their long hair on floating roofs and
I'm suddenly a pitch perfect proletariat with
a Latin dancing chauffeur and an operatic
sidekick. We sing, *every dog has his day / and
it's my turn to bite/ I'm not going away / let
the critics fly a kite* (Disney version). There
should be black tie affairs for new books
of poems. Instead of rabid paparazzi,
I've been shot at when mistaken for
a cocked cousin who died months earlier.
Where I come from, this is a comedy.

❧

Adiós false west, and I take home
souvenirs that may prevent the plane
from taking off. I tired of parties
where I hung out with valets and where
I was stalked by percentage addicts.
All business, all the time. Everyone is
somebody and anonymity a disease
that needs celebrity fundraisers. Adiós
sweet crazies who knew how to read
Tarot cards upside down to make sure
they were getting their money's worth.
I let go of all illusions, but they in turn,
won't let me go as we flee from meetings
for meetings for meetings for meetings.
The mantra was "pitch something" and
I thought of pitchers, pitchforks, pitch dark
in the city of stars. Tricksters without
myths are tragic and as balm for them
I wrote, *fire and the rose are one.* A studio
said, *it's not in the budget.* It's the perfect
ending, and that's all folks, no sequel.

Slow Change (from *Same-Sex Séances*)

I thought, it's done, I'm out.
My father died, the women in
my life married, my bed got
busy, and I wore no scarlet G.
Waitresses hit on me, sorry
I'm. Employers googled me,
so you're. I hired a skywriter,
yes I'm. I took out ads, I'm.

❧

Sometimes I remember the closet:
that spiritual corset, that cruel jock,
telephone/confessional booth, coffin
for dark rehearsals, tomb without
a name, bomb shelter inside my mind.
Sometimes I forget the closet and
step outside into the world. Men look
at me, *are you?* Yes, I'm not an idea.

The Defense of Marriage

*In Santana and Michelle Branch's music video for
"The Game of Love," couples kiss throughout—except for
same sex couples. Once again, we must rewrite the world.*

The spirit of Jean Genet brushes off
dirt as he dances out of the grave.
He's overdressed in a wicked wink.

Every time he passes men, they run
towards each other and kiss, kiss, kiss.
Golden ripples ride across the world.

The pairings are just by chance: who's
walking where, who's lingering in love's
democratic sunlight, who's just there.

Coupling are a biker and Bible salesman;
sailor and tailor; lawyer and an illegal alien;
low-rider and low-rider; baker and thief.

Jean has his arms spread open to the world,
and then the men start kissing more and
more men: threeways, orgies, dancing mobs.

Sex, but no wedding is the 11th commandment
for us, legally-defined Sodomites, sinners
in designer angst. One young man in

psychic Speedos and nerd glasses runs
on a Caribbean beach looking for any man
to kiss—but he's too shy to join any group.

He stumbles and looks up: a UFO rushes
to land by him. Out come the dead:
James Dean, Ramón Navarro, Monty Clift,

Jim Morrison, Rudolph Valentino, Sal Mineo,
James Baldwin, Reinaldo Arenas (no, no rest
for you in my poetry!). It's a family reunion.

They kiss him—some as lovers, as brothers,
as friends, as real human beings. Just for
the hell of it, let's put our Santana to play

his guitar on a pink yacht while Michelle
twirls on deck in a tuxedo: suddenly mermen
bubble up, kissing. Jean rides a dolphin and

and then looks up: the sun and the moon
rush to kiss each other. It's the end of
the world! That's how much power we have.

You, You, You

You arrive tomorrow
and I'm proud to be

no one in this myopic
bookstore on the verge

of inked bankruptcy.
I think of literate fires

in Milton, Marx, and
Marvel Comics. Today,

God seems generous
as I shop for condoms,

lubricant, poems from
Finland, French bread,

and roses unashamed
of their fragile nakedness.

All these starry books are
the opposite of graves,

islands without borders,
rooms welcoming winds.

You will soon translate me
in your arms, your yes.

Salsa Capitalism

Friends say, write a poem for J-Lo
and it's career suicide, kamikaze
loco. So—this one is for her, my J-Lo.

We're both here by sheer will, our unstill
spirits distilled into steppingstones.
Permission from who? And for what?

She's wealthy and I live on a teacher's
salary but salsa capitalism isn't about
money or a trickle-down theory of

Lorca's *duende*. It's about hearing
music to be spent inside our bodies,
rhythms' richness, the dancing, our

now foreign tears' rum, free will that's
not taxed, kingdom come as crumbs,
declamations disguised as questions,

or supple street corners mystery plays.
I never need to meet J-Lo. It must be
tiring to be an idea, a hoarded cocktail

story, Helen of Troy's ghost in San Juan,
or a music video Sor Juana. It's not
survival that counts, but the thriving.

My love don't cost a thing—just everything
that you have and what an audit can't find.
The current slowly becomes currency.

I must also strip off my expensive clothes
and run into the sea to wear salt, that
honest jewelry that I can't leave my heirs

who must misspend themselves and
come to doubt the words, *what's Cesar's
is Cesar's.* J-Lo, Jenny from the block,

Selena's döppleganger, fellow future
footnote, beautiful economist, she who
sings to remember that younger girl

who wanted it all, not knowing what
that meant. I was recently alone in
my house and danced to her music

to feel rich as my poor ghosts joined me:
Uncle Rachel, Abuela, Reuben, Little Joe,
Ralph, Aunt Sylvia, Pepe, my still anonymous

AIDS line dancers, Terri, clumsy students
that I couldn't pull back from the void,
kin that kindled me, Buzz, my lost Miguel

and other sexy alchemists that I've bedded.
We all had money to burn and wore our
earned fevers like stolen glorious crowns.

excerpts from

The Roswell Poems

1. Enter The Cowboy

Mac Brazel and a 7-year old child
find a debris field full of shine.

He's Jonah choosing a pickup truck
and not a ship as his escape from visions.

This crash has done the impossible:
it has sent ripples through a desert.

Mac returns home without absolutes.
The Proctors ask, is this sky flotsam?

One "little sliver" of silver can't be cut
or burned; he calls it memory foil.

The unknown exists without our
permission—how is that possible?

Chaves County is suddenly full of aliens
that don't speak Spanish, don't linger.

Mac's solar plexus has an eclipse.
Our cowboy tries to sleep but hears his

horses beg to be ridden where darkness
turns silver hooves into hard sparks.

2. Back To The Scene Of The Cosmic Crime

The Cowboy is in an airplane,
                    suddenly an aerial bloodhound.
Mac is godeyed without training.
                    Look for shininess. Look for
a pillaged landscape, disturbed sand.
              .   Brazel sees a Joseph and Mary
and son crossing the desert
                    (¿José, María and singing niño?).
He won't give them up to the enemy,
                    ah, to his own army. A simple
gesture: *Look, over there, it's unkempt*
                    and the plane banks to the right.
His mirage is safe, for now, and Mac
                    learns innocence is not a legal right,
that the debris field will never be
                    decoded, that his story is no longer his.

3. Visible Souvenirs

for Marguerite Helmers

Yes, there is the business of selling
the rewritten past. We *need* endless

amounts of alien-with-lit-eyes pens.
All pilgrimages are defined by

pensiveness and one's expenses.
Once, Jesus' foreskin was sold in Europe,

many times and in many places.
Our script is about Doubting Thomas'

hard change of heart as we cling
to our incredulity until conversion.

Now, alien festivals in Roswell,
Mardi Gras for the mystery addicts,

a Day of the Dead for star visitors.
Tours, lures, impure science, sureties

that we're not alone in the implied cosmos,
unashamed of shaming governmental acts.

In the past. In the present now the past.
Others wait to be abducted, singled out.

Others just buy the T-Shirt that brags,
This cowboy can beat up your astronaut.

Don Quixote Goes to The Moon

It too has long been emptied of
cantos and crusades. He likes how
his armor feels like a sigh here.

He hunts the grim ghost called
The Man on the Moon, the king of
tides and madmen's brain waters,

the thief who adorns himself
with the sun's fineries. Evil isn't
confined merely to Spain, Earth

or the human soul. A widow
offers a crater picnic and he accepts
as chivalry requires him to do.

A rover flies them to a dull valley
with views of the Void. His small
spacesuit is dull, a pliable coffin.

The widow grins and suddenly
floats away, a winged spy sent from
cruel constellations! Don Quixote

looks for a horse of any kind, but
the solar winds will not bear him.
He must crawl and curse back to

the colony! Satan, he cries out,
I will keep my eye on Earth's blue
and know the Savior's triumph

over the desolation of fecund
nothingness. Don Quixote needs
his Sancho Panza, so his thin

shadow must do. Loneliness is
a weapon in the wrong hands.
He nears the colony when suddenly

a ship hovers above him and sends
light rays to lift him to their protection.
He's illegal! And sent back to Earth

to a prayerful Spain trapped in its past.
He looks up—the Diablo of the Moon
is grinning, as if the battle is over now.

Don Quixote has a purpose again!
When you go to the stars, he tells his
pueblo, know the war with Giants

is an ancient one. He returns to the Moon
and vanishes—by his own good will?
Mystery is the food reserved for martyrs.

The Buried Sea

We're always in motion, running
ahead of the flood or fleeing winged
sharks—the sea's crudest angels.

There is always roar in our lives,
always invisible shores. We hope for
higher ground and aerial days.

Endless blue rain washes our
fingerprints off the world we love,
our claims now theoretical.

We call out each other's names
as we run, as we run, as we run.
Oxygen is our wealth, muscle ache

is practical prophecy, and breath
is the good gondolier who knows
how to respect revengeful tides.

We see fewer and fewer people
as we jump from island to island
and turn pensive peninsulas into

question marks. Storms are sent as
forged love letters, bribed border guards,
dangerous lovers, or blind spies.

Living inland for these years hasn't
kept us safe because the buried sea
never stays buried for very long.

All around us, waves collect debts that
we thought dreams. Noah's genius was in
knowing when now was the right *now*.

We shiver under the weeping moon,
watch the mountains we're running to
sink, and turn burning boats into stars.

But what of our poems? We read them
aloud to smuggle them out as echoes.
Rain and tears wash away our books.

Unlike Prospero, we've nowhere to go.
Now and soon the sea will bury us
and we will no longer be fluent in *light*.

Almost A Prayer

I no longer use my lost childhood's
simple math, no more two by two
parading before Noah's solemn eye.
We've sent a starship into space with

rudimentary summaries of Earthly life:
stick figures as naked Adam & Eve,
a raw recording of human languages,
and even maps to where we suspect

our planet dangles in zero's skies.
What was left out, what was too heavy
to escape Earth's gravity: asymmetry,
assassinations, line dancing, our need

to rebel, the coyote's loud truths, and
the Spanish Armada become driftwood.
I launch this imaginary ark of my words
and may it not become another ghost ship.

Acknowledgments

Individual magazines have been thanked and recognized in each published book; their support of my poems has been invaluable. I also wish to thank my book publishers again:

Poetry Collections: Bilingual Press/Arizona State University Press; BkMk Press/University of Missouri at Kansas City; JVC Press; University of Arizona Press/Camino del Sol Series; WordFarm Press; and Zoland Books.

Chapbooks: Ahadada Press; Anaconda Press; Last Minute Press; New Sins Press; Stonewall Books; and Sonora Review/University of Arizona.

"Early Poems" include poems published in small magazines, a world with unflagging support for younger writers. Some of these works were in: *Caliban, The Comstock Review, Empathy, Farmer's Market, Kaleidoscope, POESída* (Anthology edited by Carlos Rodriguez Matos: Ollantay Press), and *Whispering Palm Review*.

The Heath Anthology of American Literature: Volume E: Contemporary Period included four of my poems: "My Transvestite Uncle Is Missing," "Caribbean Braille," "Write What You Know," and "That Flag." I thank Dr. Lawrence La Fountain-Stokes for the lucid introduction to my poetry.

Some of the works in "Ghost Island: New Poems" were published in earlier versions and sometimes under different titles:

"The Buried Sea:" *Mid-American Review*.

"Don Quixote Goes To The Moon." Title poem to chapbook (Ahadada Press). Many thanks to Jesse Glass.

"False West: Hollywood Poems:" *Xavier Review.*

"Guardian Spirit." *#1:* Spelman College's *FOCUS.*

"Ghost Island" sections appeared in: *Buckle &, Beloit Poetry Review* (reprinted in *Poetry Daily, The Caribbean Writer, A Fi We Time: Contemporary Caribbean Lesbian and Gay Writing,* Duke University Press, edited by Thomas Glave.)

Excerpts from *The Roswell Poems.* WordFarm Press.

"Slow Change" (from *Same-Sex Séances*). *Bryant Literary Review.* Also selected for the anthology *Best Gay Poems of 2008* by A Midsummer Night's Summer's Press.

About the Author

Rane Arroyo is a gay Latino writer who is the author of seven poetry books: *Home Movies of Narcissus* (University of Arizona Press); *Pale Ramón* (Zoland Books); *The Singing Shark* (Bilingual Press/Arizona State University Press); *Columbus's Orphan* (JVC Press); *The Portable Famine* (BkMk Press/University of Missouri-Kansas City); *The Roswell Poems* (WordFarm Press) and *Same-Sex Séances* (New Sins Press). His book of fiction is *How To Name A Hurricane* (University of Arizona Press).

Arroyo was born in Chicago and began his writing career as a performance artist; he fell in love with the writing aspects of his works. Although he published his first poem at the age of 14, Arroyo began seriously working on his poems in the 1980s. He also has written numerous plays that have been performed in major U.S. cities and internationally.

He has won the 2004 Gwendolyn Brooks Poetry Prize, the John Ciardi Poetry Prize for *The Portable Famine,* the prestigious 1997 Carl Sandburg Poetry Prize for his book *The Singing Shark,* and a 1997 Pushcart Prize for a poem published in *Ploughshares.* Other awards include the Stonewall Books National Chapbook Prize for *The Naked Thief*; The Sonora Review Chapbook Contest Award for *The Red Bed*; The George Houston Bass Award for the play, "The Amateur Virgin;" the Hart Crane Memorial Award, and an Ohio Arts Council Excellence In Poetry Grant. Arroyo is included in the *Heath Anthology of American Literature: Volume E, Contemporary Period: 1945 to the present.*

He is currently a professor of Creative Writing and Literature at the University of Toledo where he is the Director of the Creative Writing Program. Arroyo has also been a Board Member and Vice-President of the Association of Writers and Writing Programs (AWP).